DONE TO DEATH IN DERBYSHIRE

Bridge End, Bradwell

DONE TO DEATH IN DERBYSHIRE

SIX HISTORIC TRUE CRIME STORIES BY
RICHARD LITCHFIELD

COUNTRY BOOKS

Published by Country Books
Courtyard Cottage, Little Longstone, Bakewell, Derbyshire DE45 1NN
Tel: 01629 640670
e-mail: dickrichardson@countrybooks.biz
www.countrybooks.biz
www.sussexbooks.co.uk

ISBN 978-1-910489-76-5

British Library Cataloguing in Publication Data.
A catalogue record for this book is available from the British Library.

Cover illustration:
The Derby Tragedy pictured in the Police News.
(See page 25)

Printed and bound in England by 4edge Ltd. Hockley, Essex
Tel: 01702 200243

DEDICATION

My beautiful daughters,
Laura and Margot.

CONTENTS

MATLOCK'S CHAMBERPOT MURDER
THE REVEREND JULIUS BENN,
MATLOCK, MARCH 5TH 1883

n the afternoon of Tuesday, 27 February 1883, two men stepped down from the London train onto the platform of Matlock Bridge Railway Station. No one could have suspected it, not even the two men, but the scene was set for one of Matlock's most bloody and senseless murders, and they were to be the principal characters in the tragedy that was played out.

To the casual onlooker there was nothing out of the ordinary about the new arrivals, and even the most keen-eyed observer would have noted only that both were respectably and soberly dressed, that the older man appeared to be in better health than his frail-looking companion, and that he seemed to be concerned for the young man to the point of taking charge of all their travel arrangements and decisions. This, however, was not an unusual sight in Matlock at the time, for it was the heyday of hydropathy in the small Derbyshire town, pioneered by local industrialist John Smedley. In hydros which had sprouted up all over the steep hillside of nearby Matlock Bank illnesses were reputedly cured by applying water to the body in a variety of ways, and 'Doctor Matlock' as the town was called by some, brought many an invalid, often with an attendant, to breathe the clean, country air and try 'the water cure'.

The older of the two men was the Reverend Julius Benn, a Congregational minister, pastor of the Old Gravel Lane Meeting House, St. Georges-in-the-East, London, for the last fifteen years. Although he was fifty-eight years old the Revd. Benn was still muscular and powerfully built, six feet in height, a crusading

Christian who believed in direct action rather than vague sermonizing He gave so frequently and generously to the poor he worked amongst, in an area described by Charles Dickens as 'a squalid maze of streets, courts and alleys… a wilderness of dirt, rags and hunger…' (1) that he was often in want himself, and family and friends had to take up collections amongst themselves to relieve Julius of his debts. Not fearing to tread where he thought the application of Christian principles was needed, both he and his third son, William, did sterling missionary work in the slums and opium dens which were so rife in the East End of London at that time. Charles Dickens, who himself did much through his writings to urge more humane treatment of the poor and downtrodden, knew Julius Benn through a home for destitute boys Julius and his wife Ann had opened, and said of him, 'One could see by the expression of the man's eye and by his kindly face that Love ruled rather than Fear, and Love was triumphant.' (1)

Julius Benn had also campaigned for penal reform and was particularly concerned that special 'reform schools' should be set up. When the first of these was built at Tiffield in Northamptonshire in 1856, Julius Benn had been placed in charge, and discharged his duties well until he left in 1863. A story told of him highlighted his Christian attitude towards his charges. When a

William Rutherford Benn as a young man

visiting governor, surveying some of the young inmates said to Julius, 'So, Mr. Benn, these are the little criminals?' Julius replied, 'No sir, these are the young *gentlemen!*'

There seems to have run through the Benn family a strong commitment to the welfare of others less fortunate and a keen sense of social duty, and this family tradition was shown in Julius's son John Williams Benn, who entered politics, became a London councillor, later an MP and was made a baronet. John's son William became an MP and was later made

Viscount Stansgate, and Julius's great grandson, Tony Benn, was a member of parliament for many years, and finished his career as M.P. for the nearby town of Chesterfield from 1984 to 2001.

The young man who accompanied Julius Benn to Matlock was his third son, William Rutherford Benn. Indeed, he was the reason for the two men being in the town out of season, for he had recently suffered a severe nervous breakdown, and had been brought away by his father to recuperate.

William was twenty-eight years old, slender, with a bushy, dark brown beard and moustache. Highly intelligent he had a gift for languages and he also wrote prose and poetry, drawing his inspiration from the romantic art movement of the day known as the Pre-Raphaelites. He was training to be a silk merchant with a firm of East Indies traders in the City of London, and spent much of his spare time working amongst the poor of Wapping and Hackney, where he was known for being notably generous to the needy.

His breakdown was sudden. On 16th December 1882, only two months prior to his arrival in Matlock, William had married Florence Nicholson, three years younger than himself, an academic young woman who greatly admired his poetry – some even said at the time that she loved the poetry more than the poet! She was an unsuitable wife for one such as William, being immature and of a melancholic disposition. He older sister Bessie, who had cared for her and protected her since the death of their parents, knew just how close to losing her own sanity Florence was on occasions. Ominously, another sister had committed suicide by drowning some years earlier. What Bessie thought of the marriage to William is not known, but she supported her sister as usual, being bridesmaid and witness at the ceremony.

As may have been predicted, the couple were totally unprepared for the physical side of marriage; the honeymoon in Paris was a disaster, and William's medical report later showed that failure to consummate their marriage led to his breakdown. The young husband fell into fits of deep depression. There were bouts of 'un-usual excitement and irritability,' and shortly after the couple's return from Paris, William was admitted into Bethnal House Asylum, East London, showing signs of violence. He was diagnosed as suffering from what the doctors termed 'mental exhaustion'. Florence returned home to Bessie at their home in Wimbledon, where she spent much of her time reading and re-reading William's verses.

In a matter of weeks there was such an improvement in William's condition that the doctors thought a convalescent spell in the country might help him further, and he was released into his father's care, with the recommendation that William and Florence should live apart for the time being. It was decided that Julius, who had come directly from nursing cholera sufferers to care for William, would take his son away to Matlock, an ideal spot as it was out of season and would be quiet and restful. William could take long walks with his father, a pursuit both enjoyed, and there would be little chance so far from London of meeting anyone who knew them and might gossip. Florence readily approved of the plan, telling Bessie that the place was 'A Gothic paradise, dripping with fantasy.' (2) Almost as if dealing with two children Bessie and Julius Benn had promised the newly weds that if William continued to improve, Florence might be able to join her husband and his father in Matlock later.

After making enquiries in Matlock for a small, quiet boarding house, the Benns arrived at The Cottage at the bottom of Steep Turnpike in the centre of town. It still stands today, with additions, opposite the Matlock Library, which was then known as The Firs, and belonged to the auctioneer, Mr. George Else. It was later renamed Harley House, presumably because of the notoriety it was to gain.

The Cottage was rented by Mary Ann Marchant and her husband, George. For many years he had been coachman to Mrs. Smedley at Riber Castle, the Victorian folly standing on a hill above Matlock and built by the man who brought hydropathy to Matlock just a few decades ago, Joseph Smedley. For the past ten months, however, the Marchants, who were described as a 'Godly and properly Christian couple,' (2) had, with Mary's elderly mother, a Mrs. Julian, lived at The Cottage, where they offered accommodation to visitors, while George also owned and operated a hackney carriage. The filled-in archway where the carriage was stored can still be clearly seen on the side of The Cottage.

The Cottage, Steep Turnpike Matlock, J. Benn murdered in room, top left window

The Reverend Benn was satisfied with the accommodation offered and engaged a sitting room and two bedrooms. He requested, soon after settling in, that William's bed be moved into his own, saying to the Marchants, 'If you don't mind removing the bed out of my son's room into mine I'll pay you the same – my son's been unwell, but is better now.' (3)

As the house was quite small this also ensured that no further guests could intrude on their privacy. When asked how long they would be staying Revd. Benn said he was uncertain, and while their tea was being prepared, the Benns took a short walk around the town, no doubt noting the many buildings arising on all sides as the boom of hydropathy continued to bring people and prosperity to what had been a small settlement on the banks of the River Derwent.

For their part the Marchants were immediately impressed by the Benns, agreeing that they appeared 'most devoted, a very Jacob and Joseph (an Old Testament father and son, famed for their attachment to each other).' (3) The affection shown by the two men for each other was most touching and noticeable to all, Julius habitually addressing his son as 'Willie, dear.' Mrs. Marchant was so pleased to have a 'gentleman of the cloth' staying at her house that she placed under the Revd. Benn's bed a family heirloom, a Blue Worcester Spode chamberpot which had belonged to her grandmother. George Marchant later recalled that 'there had been nothing uncommon in the conduct of either gentlemen,' (3) yet at the same time noted that William appeared to talk to himself and quoted frequently at length from the Bible. The landlord seems to have excused this apparent contradiction by taking into account the strong religious convictions of the two visitors.

Whilst staying at The Cottage the Benns lived quietly and, keeping in mind the need for secrecy, Julius asked specifically that their names were not to appear in the list of visitors to Matlock which was published weekly. Indeed, although they were later described as being 'chatty and sociable', they did not disclose their surnames or addresses in London.

Taking the following day, a Wednesday, to rest after their journey, the Benns then began to take gentle exercise in the form of walks in the area. Although the weather had been bad in early February, with heavy rain and gales across the Midlands, it had improved for their stay. There was little rain, and though the weather was cold, the wintry sun shone for several hours each day – ideal walking weather. On the Thursday they went by train to Buxton and walked back from there as far as Millers Dale. The following day they walked up the hill to Riber Castle and then visited the Matlock Caverns, and on the Saturday they caught the train from Matlock Bridge to Cromford, walking back via Matlock Bath and climbing the steep path to the Heights of Abraham.

That evening at five o'clock they took tea and then wrote letters, William writing to his beloved Florence, and including a poem he had written while at Matlock, its subject being an icicle-clad waterfall they had seen. They then stepped out to post the letters. Supper was at nine, the usual time at the Marchants, and when Mrs. Marchant took it in to the guests in their sitting room, she saw that William Benn was lying on the sofa, and remarked to him, 'You look tired, sir,' to which the young man said, 'Yes, I am – very.' Julius said, as they sat down to steak and kidney pie, with a treacle and suet pudding to follow (which Mrs. Marchant told them would keep out the cold!), 'We are both tired and shall retire presently.' (3)

Shortly after, father and son went to bed up the narrow, winding stairs. Julius Benn asked if he should turn out the oil light in the sitting room before they went, but Mrs. Marchant said that she would do it after she had cleared away the supper things. The Revd. Benn had only just got upstairs when he called down and asked for his son's topcoat, as there was a bottle containing a sleeping draught in one of the pockets which William took each night. After that no more was heard from the Benns that night.

*　*　*　*　*

The following morning, Sunday, March 5th, was a glorious spring day, with clear blue skies and bright sunshine. At about seven o'clock, as Mrs Marchant was preparing to rise, she heard a noise which she later found hard to describe, saying that it was 'peculiar,' a jarring, thumping sound, 'as of a pestle or something of the kind striking against a boot.' (4) She immediately though that it was her mother, who occupied a bedroom below the Marchants, knocking for attention.

Julius Benn had been most particular that his son was not to be

William Rutherford Benn,
around the time he murdered his father

woken too early and fearing that her guests might be disturbed by the noise, Mrs. Marchant hastened downstairs to her mother's room. On entering she said, 'Oh, Mother, have you been rapping? You will waken those gentlemen.' (4) Mrs Julian was most surprised and assured her daughter that she had not knocked and so, with breakfast for five to prepare, the landlady put it from her mind. She did not realise until later that she had heard a murder being committed.

The guests were early risers, being up by eight o'clock most mornings of their stay, so when by eight-thirty she had seen no sight of them, Mrs. Marchant decided to give them a call. Climbing the stairs, she knocked on the bedroom door, calling out, 'Breakfast's ready, sir.'

From the other side of the door, which Julius Benn always locked and bolted from inside upon retiring for the night, she later testified she heard a low noise, as if someone had said "m-m," almost a moan. Mrs. Marchant presumed that it was Julius Benn, warning her that William was still asleep and that he wanted him to sleep on undisturbed, so she went downstairs quietly. Suspecting nothing, she and her husband 'appropriated to their own use two eggs which had been boiled and substituted two others, observing that the gentlemen would be down directly and would like them warm.' [3] After breakfast George Marchant, having lit a fire in the parlour for the guests, went off to chapel.

As the morning wore on Mrs. Marchant became more concerned about the Benns' failure to appear. Not knowing what to do, she went frequently to the foot of the stairs and listened for any sound that might indicate that father and son were rising. On three more occasions she knocked at the bedroom door. On the second occasion she thought she heard someone saying very softly "Hush! Hush!" and the sound of someone breathing very hard, as if still asleep.

By midday Mrs. Marchant was very concerned indeed. Two letters had arrived for Julius Benn, and so she made some tea and went upstairs with this and the mail on a tray. Knocking on the bedroom door she called out, "Will you take a cup of tea, sir?" (3) but only received the same unintelligible reply once more. She did not like to try the door, and not knowing what else she could do, she left the tea and letters on the mat outside the bedroom door and went downstairs to await the return of her husband from chapel.

George Marchant did not come straight home from chapel, and so Mrs. Marchant had to wait another uneasy hour before he returned. When he did finally enter the house, she put the problem into his hands immediately.

"George, those gentlemen have not come down," she told him.

"You had better go up and see if there is anything wrong. If you go up perhaps they will open the door to you." (3)

Little suspecting the horror he was about to face George did as his wife asked him. He went upstairs, knocked twice, called out, but received no answer. He knocked again, asking more loudly through the closed door, "Is anything amiss?" (5)

At this he heard the door being unbolted from the other side, and the scene which met the coachman's eyes as the door was opened by William Benn was described graphically by a newspaper of the time:

"The young man who had unbolted the door stood silent and erect in front of him in his night dress, his throat, beard hands, night dress, legs and feet dripping with blood…" (4)

*   *   *   *   *

As Marchant stood, transfixed, William Benn turned in the doorway and silently pointed towards the bed behind him, its foot nearest the door. The horrified landlord looked, and saw Julius Benn lying there, with the right side of his head smashed in, The room was literally a shambles, with blood everywhere, on the walls and windows, on the wash stand, the looking glass and pictures, on the floor and ceiling, as well as the bed on which the murdered man lay.

Fearing that William Benn might attack him next, George Marchant hastily pulled the door to, and ran downstairs. He bundled his wife and her mother out through the door and into the yard outside, shouting excitedly, "Come out! Come out! The son has murdered his father! He will perhaps murder you!" (6)

William Benn made no attempt to come downstairs, however, so, leaving wife and old lady to watch the house, the landlord ran across the road to the Firs, home of George Else, the auctioneer, who was just sitting down with his family to their Sunday dinner. Else sent his two sons for the police and medical assistance, then accompanied Marchant back across the road to guard the house. Within ten minutes of the grim discovery first being made, Dr. Moxon, his assistant, Dr. Hunter, and Police Constable Frederick Smith arrived on the scene.

Not knowing what to expect, but prepared for a violent

confrontation, the three men warily entered The Cottage and climbed the stairs. P.C. Smith tried the closed door and found it to be locked once more. He knocked and there came the sound of the bolt being drawn back.

William, still in his bloodstained nightgown, opened the door and then turned away, walking over to the window. As the three men entered the room and approached him, it became obvious that he was wounded too, and that a large amount of the blood he was covered in came from a wound on his neck. A small, horn-handled penknife lay on the dresser, blade open, and it was with this that the young man had attempted to cut his throat at some time in the morning. He was still bleeding from the wound, and was weak from loss of blood, possibly one reason why he had made no attempt to escape from the room.

Dr. Moxon cautiously greeted William, who made no reply. While P.C. Smith fetched a chair, Moxon asked the man how he felt, but William still did not answer. At this the constable put the chair down, and without offering the slightest resistance, William Benn sat in it. Smith pinioned William's arms from behind, and Moxon set about the stitching the cut in the man's throat, the wound proving upon close inspection to be relatively small, only about an inch in length (2·5cm).

The *Derbyshire Times* describes what the doctor and police had to deal with in horrific detail: 'Sergeant Gee came upon the scene at this stage and the body of the elder gentleman was examined and found to be quite dead – one side of the head and neck being quite a shapeless mangled mass. The brain was protruding, and the room was in a state which defies description.' (4)

Despite this, the reporter went on to describe it: "The room is not a large one and the two ordinary sized bedsteads did not leave very much space – the beds not being parallel. Deceased's bed foot was towards the door, and the son's bed-head near the window overlooking the Chesterfield road (Steep Turnpike), with a beautiful south-west prospect. Near the window, two yards from deceased's bed was a dressing table on which a looking-glass stood, and that glass and the window panes were stained with blood. The ceiling was similarly bespattered; over deceased's bedhead hung two prints, "The Lord's Supper," and a companion print, and the subjects were scarcely discernible for the fact that the glass was so coated with blood – and yet strange to say, they were hanging quite a yard directly above deceased's head. In the corner facing the window stood a washstand with the water and usual provisions for washing, and the basin, stand and jug were like the other articles covered with blood although quite at the opposite side of the room to the window and four yards away. The ceiling, walls, and in fact almost everything in the room were similarly sprinkled, while the bed and floor were in a far worse condition, and everything went to show the powerful violence the murderer had exercised on his poor victim." (4)

Floorboards below the bed were saturated with Julius's blood and had to be later replaced, and an elderly man told the author during research for this account how, when he went to live at The Cottage in the 1920's, he was told this detail by the man whose father had redecorated the murder room. The boy located the actual room where the murder was done by lifting all the carpets in all the upstairs rooms when his parents were elsewhere, until he found a section of newer floorboards in one of them. When the house came up for sale some years ago, this detail could still be seen in an upstairs bedroom.

Once William's wound had been attended to, Constable Smith gave took him into an adjoining room, where he sat still not speaking and described as being 'vacant', (4) with a blanket wrapped around him, supervised by the constable. In the room next door Doctors Moxon and Hunter set about the grisly task of examining the body of Revd. Julius Benn.

Doctor Moxon later testified at the inquest that Julius Benn appeared to have been murdered in his sleep. The corpse lay on its left side; all the injuries were to the right side of the head, and one newspaper reported that 'The hands of the aged gentleman were by his side, further evidence that no struggle for life had taken place.' [4] Two weapons had been used: a heavy, blunt object to bludgeon the victim, and a knife to sever the vulnerable arteries, though Julius was probably already dead from the first onslaught.

Sergeant Gee arrived whilst Moxon and Hunter were still conducting their examination of the corpse. Leaving P.C. Smith to continue guarding William Benn, Gee searched the bedroom for the weapons with which the minister had been killed. The front garden of The Cottage below the Benns' bedroom window was also searched in case William had thrown a weapon out earlier. Nothing was found. Back in the murder room, Dr. Moxon indicated the small, brown handled penknife on the dresser with which the secondary wounds had apparently been inflicted, and then, after further searching, Sergeant Gee drew from under the plain iron bedstead on which the body lay the weapon that had caused such extensive, horrific wounds. It was the prized blue chamberpot with which Mrs. Marchant had favoured her guests. Apart from a small chip on one edge it had been undamaged in the frenzied attack. Covered with blood inside and out, and with hair from the victim still adhering to it, it was clearly the heavy, blunt weapon which the police sergeant had been looking for. A thorough person however, Gee continued his search of the room, and found hidden under the carpet a purse with seven pounds in gold coins in it. It is a bitter irony that Julius Benn should so distrust the Marchants that he concealed his money and at night secured the bedroom door against them, only to lock himself in with someone who would take something far more valuable than a few paltry pounds from him while he slept.

Sergeant Gee felt that he had enough evidence to charge William Benn with murder, and stepping back into the bedroom he did so, cautioning William that anything he said would be given in evidence. Benn still said nothing, but 'drew a long breath'.

By this time the news had quickly spread around the town, and as a paper of the day records it, 'hundreds of residents and visitors were on the spot, eagerly gleaning what particulars they could, many people being under the impression that the case was merely one of suicide, and only the few who from curiosity found their way into the bedroom were "rewarded" by the most ghastly sight that could possibly have been witnessed formed any true idea of the shocking nature of the case.' (4) Needless to say, those ghouls who did force their way onto the scene of such a tragedy quickly retreated, leaving the cramped room to the professionals who were busy there.

Sergeant Gee took charge of the prisoner and sent Constable Smith on a long walk to the town of Wirksworth, five miles away, to the office of the police division there, where he was to inform Superintendent Sharpe of the murder. In the meantime, as the Benns had not disclosed their addresses to the Marchants, Gee collected together all the mail which the father and son had received during their stay.

When Superintendent Sharpe arrived from Wirksworth he opened one of the letters which had been delivered that very day. It was from the dead man's sister in London, saying that she hoped they were 'getting on well,' and that she 'was glad to hear they had such nice lodgings.' (7) She also advised, too late for poor Julius, that he call someone else in if he felt that he needed help in caring for William. This letter provided the police with the information needed in order to contact relatives of the Benns, and a telegram was sent that afternoon, informing the Benn family in London of the death of Julius Benn.

It was decided by the police that there was little point in interrogating William Benn that day, and later in the afternoon Doctor Moxon authorised William's removal to Derby Infirmary, 21 miles distant. A cab and a pair of horses were hired, and with the prisoner inside, guarded by P.C. Smith and Sergeant Gee, they set off for Derby. The prisoner spoke on several occasions to his guards during the journey, but made no admission of guilt, or even reference to the murder.

Arriving at Derby Infirmary at seven-thirty that evening, the police were reminded by the hospital authorities that they would not take charge of William Benn unless there was a police guard at the bedside at all times, a regulation in force whenever an attempted suicide or other prisoner needed medical attention. Sergeant Gee left P.C. Smith in charge of the prisoner whilst he went to arrange for police guards with the Derby police force, and at about ten o'clock that night William Benn finally confessed to the murder, saying to Smith, "I did it with the chamber utensil." (4) Asked at the inquest by a juror how Benn seemed when making the confession, the constable replied that 'prisoner seemed unconcerned and not at all excited. He looked rather peculiar about the eyes, and a sleepy sensation appeared to come over him.' (4)

William's wounds were examined and further attended to. He had attempted to cut his throat after killing his father, but although the windpipe was cut the larger vessels were intact, and it was predicted that he would make a complete physical recovery. The poor young man's mental health would probably never be whole again, and the pity of it is caught by a journalist, who wrote, 'From his youth he had borne an irreproachable character. He had always been attentive in the highest degree to his business duties, and his leisure moments had been devoted almost solely to intellectual pursuits and to the furtherance of the good work in which his father set him so forcible an example.' (4)

Some days later, a newspaper reported, William supposedly wrote and signed a statement saying that he committed the murder as the church clock was striking eight, but given that Mrs. Marchant almost certainly heard the murder blows being struck as she was getting up at seven a.m., and the Revd. Benn was always up and ready for his breakfast by the hour of eight during his stay at Matlock, William would appear to have miscounted the number of chimes.

* * * * *

The preliminary inquest was held the following day at the Queen's Hotel, Matlock Bridge, when the Coroner told the jury that 'they were all aware the deceased gentleman met with an untimely end on the previous day, having, it was supposed, been murdered by his son.' Until 1926 it was required that the jury view the corpse, so after they had been sworn in the somewhat apprehensive jury members made their way from the hotel and over the bridge to Steep Turnpike and The Cottage, watched by curious bystanders.

The bedroom had been cleaned up as much as was possible. The corpse had been washed and laid out on the bed, and the unpleasant task of the jurymen was aptly phrased by the *Derbyshire Times* of March 7th: 'The sight was not one easily forgotten… When the ghastly wounds were laid bare a shudder passed through all present, and even the Coroner exclaimed that 'he had never seen such a horrible case before.' (3) Several of the jurymen expressed their surprise that such a violent murder could have taken place without attracting the attention of the other people in the house. The viewing of the body completed, and the letter of the law fulfilled, the jury returned to the Queen's Hotel, to hear evidence of identification.

Charles Taylor Mycock, nephew of the deceased, a draper from Hyde in Cheshire, attested that the body was that of Julius Benn. The coroner then adjourned the inquiry until the following morning so that other representatives of the Benn family could be present.

The inquest proper was attended by five relatives and friends of the deceased, including Julius's eldest son, John William Benn, who represented the family in the proceedings. John Benn was an artist, lecturer and publisher, founder of the Benn family publishing firm, sometimes known as 'The Blindfold Sketcher' for his remarkable ability to draw from memory whilst blindfolded. He was very much his father's son, a forthright and honest man, and no respecter of authority for its own sake. He was determined to spare the family as much grief as possible whilst fighting to save William from a murder trial. Julius's wife was unable to attend, as she was an invalid, suffering from chronic dysentery, and the news of her husband's death put her close to death, while Florence, William's young wife, had collapsed and was being nursed at home by the sturdy older sister, Bessie.

The first witness called was Dr. Moxon, who testified that the injuries were all confined to the right side of the head, face and neck, that there were three wounds and the frontal and parietal and temple bones were smashed in and the right ear completely destroyed. The doctor attributed death to the extensive injures to the brain. At this stage, the coroner asked if the doctor had examined the brain, and Moxon replied that he had not. Superintendent Sharpe intervened, saying, "It is quite necessary," (4) as he had to consider the medical evidence to be submitted at any trial for murder which might follow.

John Benn rose and asked that a further postmortem on his father not be undertaken, out of respect for the body. At this he and the coroner became involved in exchanges, with the coroner saying that the medical evidence was incomplete, and John Benn trying to save his father's remains from what he was saw as any further indignities. John said he did not see 'what good it would do to stir up deceased's brains as suggested for some purpose he did not know.' (4) After Superintendent Sharpe had pointed out that an explicit statement needed to be given as to the exact cause of death, pointing out that 'Prisoner would have to go to the Assizes, and it would not do to send any imperfect evidence before the jury,' (4) Dr. Moxon left the room and went to make a further post mortem examination. When he returned half an hour later, he said that from his examinations he could positively state that death was attributable to injuries to the brain, caused by the chamberpot, and that two wounds to the ear had been caused by something sharp, probably a knife. In reply to Mr. Maycock, the deceased's nephew, he did not consider that a sharp, chipped edge to the chamberpot could have caused these wounds. Asked by a juror, he said that in his opinion the first blow would have stunned Julius Benn, and he was killed by subsequent blows. There were no signs of a struggle.

Mrs. Marchant, described patronisingly by the *Derbyshire Times* correspondent as 'a most intelligent person just past the prime of life,' (4) was then called. She told of the whole tragic chain of events, from the time that the Benns first stepped into her house to the moment when her husband forced her out of it, telling her that murder had been done. Questioned as to the conduct of the accused murderer throughout the week, Mary Marchant said that William was very quiet. She had not seen him read or write, and his conduct was that of someone who had been ill. She added, sounding as bewildered as anyone else who knew William Benn, that "…a nicer person I never met." (4) The jury complimented Mrs. Marchant on the clear and collected way she had given evidence, which they thought 'almost surprising, considering the great shock she had received.' (4)

Her Husband, William Marchant then deposed, telling of all he had seen, to be followed by the police constable, Frederick Smith, first on the scene, who testified to finding the body of Julius Benn and to later hearing William Benn confess to the act of parricide. He in turn was followed by Sergeant Robert Gee, who spoke of searching the bedroom, finding the knife, and then the chamberpot. He unwrapped the murder weapon to show pieces of hair still adhering to the underside of the rim and held it aloft for all of the room to see, causing 'quite a sensation.' (4)

Gee was still testifying when John Benn intervened again, asking that his father's effects be searched and a document from Bethnal Green Lunatic Asylum be found and submitted as evidence. This document had been given to the Reverend Benn and was authorised by the Chief Physician of the institution, releasing William into the care of his father for a period of rest in the country. John Benn argued that it was important that the jury consider the state of mind of his brother at the time of the murder, and that it was also important in considering the statement made by William, confessing to the murder of his father. Sergeant Gee said that he had possession of all the papers which belonged to the Benns which he had found at The Cottage, and the coroner allowed an adjournment for lunch in order that the paper might be found and produced as evidence. When the enquiry reconvened Sergeant Gee said that the paper in question had not been found, and the coroner, establishing that the police had no more to add to the enquiry, told the jury that that was all the evidence he proposed to call.

At this John Benn was on his feet again. He asked the coroner if it was not possible to submit 'evidence as to the state of mind of the son,' (4) and the coroner said it could not be considered. Benn pressed him. Was he sure the jury could not add a rider to their verdict? The coroner said it could not, that 'That question is a subject which will arise at a subsequent examination, should there be one.' (4) Benn was adamant and harried the coroner.

"Those statements are extremely damaging to the family," he told him. "It does seem queer that you should have the power to admit one class of evidence and suppress another." (4)

The coroner replied that it was far from his wish to suppress evidence, but that the jury were only met to decide as to the cause of death. John, knowing that his brother would face the hangman if his insanity was not proved, argued that the coroner had accepted evidence from the two policemen as to the state of mind of William Benn, but the coroner replied that his depositions only referred to the general demeanour of the prisoner, and John had to content himself with appealing to the representatives of the press to take note of his remarks and make them public, saying that it 'would assist his family and himself in their severe trouble.' (4) Shortly afterwards the coroner summed up and said that 'in the face of the evidence there could be no doubt that the deceased met his death at the hands of his son.' (4) The jury consulted for a few minutes, then brought in a verdict of wilful murder against William Benn, and he was committed to the next Derbyshire Assizes on the coroner's warrant.

For several days William was watched very closely. He called repeatedly for a knife so that he could kill himself and on occasions asked his assistants and guard to cut his head off. On the Tuesday after the murder, he was visited by his two brothers, 'and although he appeared to recognise them for a brief period, he speedily relapsed into a condition of rambling unconsciousness.' (7) On Wednesday, 14th March, whilst still at Derby Infirmary, he made another attempt at suicide.

While his guard, a P.C. Alexander was putting his boots on prior to being relieved of his duty, Benn, who had been quiet during the day '… suddenly jumped up, rushed to the window, and got through. Alexander followed, and caught him by the night shirt, but it gave way, and Benn fell to the ground, a distance of over twenty feet.' (8) In doing so, he sprained his ankle and injured his back and was 'much cut by the glass.' (8)

Meanwhile, in London, the funeral of Julius Benn took place in his own place of worship and ministry on the 8th March, and was attended by a huge congregation of mourners, whilst streets were packed by others in the predominantly poor area who wished to show their respect. Benn had not been a wealthy man, but he was well-loved by the poor among whom he had worked so selflessly for years. A reporter noted that 'In the neighbourhood of Old Gravel Lane the signs of affection were apparent on every hand.' (9) His coffin was smothered in floral tributes, and many reverend gentlemen who had known Julius attended, with over a dozen named in the papers. *The Hackney and Kingsland Gazetter* reported that: 'The way in which the poor people of the district wept around the coffin was a most affecting tribute to the memory of the departed pastor. The grief of the young people connected with Sunday School was a specially marked feature on the sad occasion.' (9)

At Julius's graveside his mentor from the days when Julius was a young man, thereafter becoming a lifelong friend, The Reverend J. Williams, the officiating minister, reminded the mourners of the words of Matthew, xxiv. 44., 'Be ye also ready; for in such an hour as ye think not the son of man cometh,' adding that it was not flattery, Julius had 'grown in grace' all his adult life, and had been prepared to meet his God. (10)

Still under care in Derby, William's mental state worsened; when he appeared for remand on the 27th March, he was described as being 'quite incoherent,' and addressed the magistrate as 'Pontius Pilate.' A subsequent remand appearance was cancelled as William's mental state rendered him unable to attend. This evidence and other proofs of his insanity resulted in proceedings against him being quashed. On April 11th, William Rutherford Benn was admitted to the Asylum for the Criminally Insane at Broadmoor, a decision which seems to have met with general approval, for three days later the *High Peak News* reported:

'Very general satisfaction will have been created by the action of the Home Secretary in saving the Matlock Murderer and his distressed relatives the ordeal of a trial. Prisoner was subjected to a keen medical examination, and the physicians came to the unanimous conclusion that there was no hope of a recovery. A copy of this testimony – which would presumably be taken in the presence of judicial authorities – forwarded to Sir William Harcourt, produced an order for the removal of the man to Broadmoor Criminal Asylum, where he will no doubt spend the rest of his unhappy days on earth.' (11)

It is not known why William decided that bright, sunny day of March 5th, 1883, to kill his father. Clearly he was deranged; today there is more chance that he would probably have been diagnosed as schizophrenic from the onset of his breakdown, his condition have been treated, and the tragedy prevented, but something triggered the senseless violence, and a comment made by Mary Marchant when testifying during the inquest, as well as testimony from the man who spent most time with William on the day he murdered his father, P.C. Smith, may give us a clue.

When explaining why she had not realised that something was badly wrong when the Benns did not come downstairs on the Sunday morning, she is reported as saying, '...she thought they would be very tired after their Saturday's long excursion, and further, she believed *that when people were very tired and took sleeping draughts they did not take effect until a long time after they were taken.'*

(author's italics). It may be recalled that Mrs. Marchant testified at the inquest that on the night before the murder Julius Benn called downstairs to her, asking that she bring upstairs the bottle containing the sleeping draught, which was in a pocket of William's topcoat, and as the *Sheffield Independent* reported, 'The health of the son was such that he could not procure sleep without the assistance of an opiate.' (2)

It is a strange paradox what while some of the Victorian middle classes were firmly teetotal (Julius and William both wore in their lapels the badge of the Blue Ribbon Army, a temperance society), they saw no harm in using, quite casually, medicines containing opium. Chemists would often make up and sell without question their own nostrums containing drugs which are strictly controlled today. Opium, with its properties of inducing vivid dreams and hallucinations, of divorcing the habitual user from reality, can also induce paranoia, and was surely the last thing that a man like William, already prone to violence and wandering in his mind and listening to imaginary voices, needed. A possible scenario for the murder is that William took a too-heavy dose of opium on Saturday night, and woke on Sunday still heavily affected by it, or a further dose early in the morning and then, under its influence, set upon Julius as he slept, what in more modern terminology could be called a 'bad trip'. P.C. Smith seems to be describing someone still in the grips of the drug when he says of William that 'prisoner seemed unconcerned and not at all excited. He looked rather peculiar about the eyes, and a sleepy sensation seemed to come over him.' (4)

*　*　*　*　*

Surprisingly, after the doctor's diagnosis, William recovered his sanity after a very short time in Broadmoor, and when this became apparent to his relatives, John Benn made strenuous efforts to get him released, though it took several years to do so. William's wife, Florence, was keen to be reunited with her husband, standing loyally by him all the time that he was in Broadmoor, writing every day of the week to him, and twice on a Sunday. In 1890, after the doctors and John had agreed that William's sanity was completely restored, John Benn contacted the Home Secretary and applied for his brother's release, guaranteeing to be personally responsible for William's conduct. It was a brave, selfless act on John's part, for he was at the time standing in a parliamentary by-election as a Liberal candidate, and any adverse publicity could have prejudiced his chances of succeeding.

John's guarantee was accepted, and William was freed. A post was found for him with an East India merchant in London, and he and Florence went to live at 15, Dornton Road in Balham. William decided that to avoid notoriety he would change his name, abandoning the surname Benn and adopting instead William's middle name of Rutherford.

All seemed to go well. The couple were happy together, and on the 11th May 1892, they became a family, when Florence gave birth to a daughter and they named her Margaret Taylor. In 1897 the Rutherford family set sail for India, where William continued his trade of silk merchant, and tended the sick and poor of Delhi and Madras. Writing of his humanitarian work, Florence told Bessie, 'William is making an earnest effort to redeem himself.' (2)

For some years the couple were extremely happy, by all reports, and this happiness seemed to be complete when Florence became pregnant again. William wished to send Florence back to England to give birth, where she could be cared for by Bessie, but Florence insisted on staying in India. As her pregnancy advanced, however, Florence's mental condition gave cause for alarm, and William telegrammed for Bessie to come out to India. Even as Bessie was packing, came another telegram. Florence was dead. Three months later William, accompanied by young Margaret, arrived at Bessie's house in Wimbledon. There in a very emotional state, he broke the awful news to her. Florence had hanged herself from a tree near their house in India one night. A

Florence Nicholson Benn,
William's wife and Margaret's mother.
Committed suicide in India

servant had found the body when dawn broke.

William had loved his wife deeply and was inconsolable. It was decided that he would return to India, to continue his trade as a silk merchant, but what was to be done with his daughter? John Benn and his wife Lily wanted to take care of her, but Florence's sister Bessie insisted on raising the child. Margaret stayed with Aunt Bessie, and Bessie passed on to her niece her own love for the theatre, so that Margaret Rutherford chose a career in acting and became one of the most successful and well-loved character actresses of both stage and screen. It is another irony of this true story that Margaret Rutherford appeared in several films whose central motif was bloody murder, being best remembered for her character portrayal of Agatha Christie's celebrated lady detective, the eccentric Miss Marple.

Sadly, the story does not finish there, for in 1902 John Benn received a letter from India which was to cause him much mental anguish. William wrote to tell him that he had met a young English woman and was engaged to be married to her. John thought long and hard, and eventually decided that as he was responsible for his brother's freedom and guarantor for his actions whilst living free, he could not in all conscience allow the marriage to go ahead without the young woman and her family knowing of William's past. He wrote to the woman's parents, telling them of the murder and William's former insanity, and the parents, not surprisingly, forbade the marriage and the engagement was broken off.

William was so incensed by what he regarded as an act of treachery on his brother's part that he immediately took ship to England to confront John. His anger was so great, and he brooded on it so deeply on the long sea journey home that he lost his sanity once more. This left John in a difficult and unenviable position, and after consulting with doctors he felt that he could no longer stand as guarantor for William, and he was committed to Northumberland House, a private asylum for the insane in Harringay. In 1904, he began to display homicidal tendencies, and was transferred to Broadmoor, where he stayed until 1921. Young Margaret was told that her father was dead, that he had died nursing the sick in India when she was still very young, and when she asked Aunt Bessie where her

Stone Asylum, where William died in 1921

father was buried, she told her, 'In the Benn family vault.' (2)

Both friends and biographers told a truly horrifying tale of how Margaret Rutherford finally learned the truth about her father. Somewhere around the year 1904, when Margaret would have been twelve or thirteen, she answered a knock at the front door of the Wimbledon home she shared with Aunt Bessie, and found a tramp on the doorstep – looking like King Lear, Rutherford was to tell friends in later years. The man said he had brought her a message from her father and Margaret told the man he was mistaken, that her father had died in India years ago. No, the man said, he is in Broadmoor and I saw him only today; he sends you his love. And with that he left, having shattered Margaret's peace of mind. Aunt Bessie told her the truth about her father, and her mother, and Margaret fell into a deep depressive breakdown. She suffered from crying fits, didn't communicate with anyone, and for the rest of her life she feared that she too might lose her mind and harm someone – or herself. In later life, particularly when the pressures of acting weighed upon her, she would take refuge in nursing homes and be cared for until she felt stronger. As a result of this contact from the father, a male relative of William asked Broadmoor that all future correspondence of William's be forwarded to him. In fairness to William, he never in any way threatened his daughter with any harm.

Grave of William and Florence Rutherford, Gap Road Cemetery, Wimbledon

In 1921, his health very poor by now, William was transferred to the City of London Asylum at Stone, near Dartford in Kent. Margaret, with the influence of the Benns, had managed to effect the move. There William suffered two strokes and was confined to an invalid carriage. On August 4th of that year, having contracted pneumonia, he died, a sad, tragic man who wrote one of the bloodiest tales in the history of Matlock.

REFERENCES

1. 'A Small Star in the East' from *The Uncommercial Traveller* by Charles Dickens, *All the Year Round Magazine 1868*, 19th December 1868.
2. *Margaret Rutherford: A Blithe Spirit* by Dawn Langley Simmons, pub. Arthur Barker Ltd., London 1983.
3. *The Derbyshire Times*, Wednesday March 7th 1883.
4. *The Derbyshire Times*, Saturday March 10th 1883.
5. *The Derbyshire Advertiser & Journal*, Friday March 9th 1883.
6. *The Sheffield & Rotherham Independent*, Tuesday March 6th 1883.
7. *The East London Observer*, Saturday March 10th 1883.
8. *The Globe*, Thursday March 15th 1883
9. *The Hackney & Kingsland Gazette*, Monday March 12th 1883.
10. *The East London Observer*, Saturday March 24th 1883.
11. *The High Peak News*, Saturday 14th April 1883.

THE DERBY TRAGEDY
LILIE BURFORD AND ROBERT FERON,
DERBY, 13TH APRIL 1889

f you had been present in Derby of 1889, and had met the two principal characters in what was called 'The Derby Tragedy' by both local and national press, it would have probably seemed to you at first sight that Lillie Burford and the young Belgian, Robert Feron were a perfect love-match. They had recently met and fallen in love with each other, and it looked as if the affair, only a couple of weeks old, would blossom. She was strikingly beautiful with 'a splendid head of golden hair', (1) and he was a handsome young man of medium height with a fashionable moustache, of a dark complexion and sharp features, a well-off young man with good prospects in life. Yet they were not 'good' for each other, for they shared a morbid obsession that was to be end of them both. That obsession was an unhealthy fascination with dying a romantic, sensational death together. They should never have met.

Robert Feron had been living in Derby for over a year when he met Lillie. He was the son of a wealthy boot manufacturer of some social standing in Brussels. His father had made the acquaintance of an Englishman whose brother had a business in Derby, a Mr Holme of Bath Street Silk Mills. Robert was sent to Mr. Holme in England with a letter of introduction, and Mr Holme agreed to give the young Belgian an unpaid post in his mill, in the foreign correspondence section. The aim was to perfect his English language skills, learn Spanish with a tutor, and gain knowledge of the silk trade in order to develop it commercially on the continent. He lodged near to the mills, in Stafford. Street with a Mr. Waterfall and family. He was given a generous allowance by his father, and 'appears to have spent a good deal of money.' (2)

At such a young age – only seventeen when he came to England – Robert seems to have kicked over the traces, and it was to prove his undoing. He was not a drinker, being described by friends as 'very abstemious', and 'almost teetotal' (3) He was, however a very accomplished dancer, and went frequently to the theatre in both Derby and Nottingham, and 'appeared to relish sensational dramatic fare.' (4) He also 'had a penchant for the society of actresses and music-hall artistes.' (5) A local newspaper said that 'It is to be feared that the lad… was what is commonly known as 'fast'. Though bountifully supplied with money, he got into debt and plunged into dissipation.' (6) Several papers reported that 'he had been leading a gay life,' (7) which does not mean what it does today, but is interesting nevertheless and has bearing on the tragedy, as shall be seen.

In temperament, Robert was usually amiable and friendly, but one (unnamed) friend said that he was 'of a very excitable and impulsive temperament… The least hitch threw him into a passion, and he had been known to indulge in a few French expletives at a private ball.' (8)

Further, Robert carried a small nickel-plated revolver, perfectly legal at that time, which he would produce and flourish to impress people. That should have been enough warning, really. An event some months previously should have been enough to send Feron home, but he seems to have escaped virtually unchecked for it. He had formed a friendship with a local merchant's daughter, and when she broke off the relationship, he confronted her with the revolver and threatened to shoot her if she did not consent to continue meeting him! Whether this was the spark that caused Mr. Holme to alert Feron's father or not we don't know, but Mr. Holme contacted him in Brussels and he 'was informed that he had better have his son at home again. The elder Feron came over but 'his son kept so close to him during his visit that no representation could be made to him, and the result was that he (Robert Feron) remained in Derby.' (9)

Lillie Burford probably met Feron at the theatre in Derby, though it is not known for sure. A native of Spennymoor in County Durham, she had been a milliner, setting up business at her parents' house, then, being fond of the stage, she joined a travelling theatrical company when she was 18 and came back with the touring company Monte Cristo in 1887 to appear on stage at the Cambridge Theatre in her home town. It was believed that her stage name was Nellie Barford. (10) The following year she gave up the stage and came home 'ill' in May. What the 'illness' was became apparent when she gave birth to an illegitimate child, a boy, in September. The child's father was called George, though his last name is not known, and he lived at Kidsgrove, near Stoke-on-Trent. According to Lillie and her family, she and George were engaged, though it seems to have been a long engagement, for by March of 1889, Lillie left County Durham, and the baby with her mother, and headed for Derby to lodge with an aunt, a Mrs. Clara Williams, who lived with her husband at 53 Prince's Street, in the Pear Tree district of Derby. They didn't seem to know about Lillie's child, only being told she had been 'ill', and was now looking for work in Derby, possibly as a barmaid or milliner. She told the Williams's that she had been an actress, 'but did not care for the stage.' (11)

Whether there had been a family row, causing Lillie to leave home, we shall not know now, but she was depressed and in low spirits when she first came to Derby, and went to the theatre to take her mind off her problems. There she met Robert Feron, it is believed, and they began a brief and intense love affair, living it out as if they were involved in some sensational Victorian melodrama of the type they had both seen on stage and in which Lillie had no doubt acted. It was almost as if they were playing parts, more in love with the drama of loving than the person they professed to love, Lillie the beautiful, doomed heroine, Robert the handsome, passionate lover dying in the bloom of youth. It was the type of sensational fare served up often (twice nightly and matinee on Saturday) in a lot of Victorian theatres, and also in the romantic novels that Lillie was addicted to reading. As the *Derby Daily Telegraph* summed it up: 'What the boy wanted was a calm, steady, strong-willed companion, instead of which he became infatuated with a girl as weak and foolish as himself.' (6) Lillie was described dismissively by one paper as 'an ultra sentimental dressmaker,' with a 'head full of maudlin nonsense.' (6) Strong stuff, but fairly accurate, it seems. Robert, a personal friend remarked, 'was never a favourite with ladies,' (8) possibly because he was still so young, and Lillie, friends said, had a beauty 'admitted by all, and she appears to have known it too well herself.' (1) It seems to have been a self-destructive mutual-admiration society that could only end badly. And it did.

* * * * *

Lillie passed Robert off to Mrs. Williams as George, her fiance from Kidsgrove, and said that he was living at St. James' Hotel in town, and had come to work at Holme's Mills as a foreign correspondence clerk, which was the job Feron was doing. Although a relative of Lillie's, Mrs. Williams did not know Lillie, nor much about her till she came to Derby, and 'George who was Robert' became a regular visitor to the house in Pear Tree. Mrs Williams seems to have accepted that 'George' was foreign because she hadn't been told differently by her sister, Lillie's mother. The Williams's took to Robert Feron, saying later that: '… they were pleased with Mr.Feron's manner. He was a jovial companion, and was generally in a very merry mood,' and they observed that 'The young couple seemed passionately fond of one another.' (9)

A great reader of what was described in several reports as 'trashy novels' or 'sensational novels', Lillie seems to have been won over by Robert's wealth and looks, his passion for dancing and the theatre. He must have seemed an exotic creature to her – rich, travelled, with cultivated manners. Small wonder that within days she had confessed to Robert that, though she was engaged to George, she preferred him! And then there was the dark flirtation with a romantic death together that became more real the more each indulged the other in their morbid fantasies of 'causing a great sensation,' (9) as Lillie put it to Mrs. Williams on one occasion.

Only a few days into her romance with the young Belgian, Lillie indicated her open neck on her dress she was wearing and said, to her landlady '"How nice it would be for a bullet to go in here." ' (12) Clara made a disparaging remark, and Lillie laughed. A few days later, Lillie laid aside a romantic novel she was reading and said to Clara Williams that 'It would be nice to die with my lover'. (12) She was reading a novel about 'a young gentleman poisoning his young lady with something in the coffee, and then said, "It would be nice to die in each other's arms." ' (12) On the Tuesday or Wednesday of their last week together when Robert and Lillie were sitting on a couch at the Williams's, Robert said, ' "I would die for you, Lillie; would you die for me?" She replied, "Yes, I would," and touched him on the side of the face." (12). Drawn together into the darkness of their morbid delusions, they fed each other's appetite for the dangerous allure of a 'romantic death.' Sadly, it is those who are left behind to pick up the pieces afterwards who can vouch there is no such thing.

The revolver featured largely in their planned death pact. One evening when Robert had called at Lilly's lodgings, Lillie asked Robert to show the Williams's his revolver, and he took it out of his pocket and flourished it. Mrs Williams said that she was surprised that Lillie wasn't afraid of him carrying it, and Lillie replied airily, "Oh, he understands it," and added that 'foreigners were accustomed to firearms.' (9) At that, Robert pointed the gun directly into Lillie's face. She did not flinch, but merely laughed at their grim game. Clara Williams, 'a worthy and practical woman', (9) asked him to put it away, as it might go off.

*   *   *   *   *

If Feron was happy with Lillie's company, he was not happy at his work. His best friend there, a Mr. D'Aubry, foreign correspondence clerk at the mill, who worked alongside Robert and had become a close friend and confidant, later testified that for the fortnight previous, the young man had been 'very gloomy', and 'paid little attention to his business.' (13) He complained of having a cold, and pains in his heart, but as will be seen, there was a lot more than a simple chill troubling Robert Feron.

On Friday of 12th April, Robert took Lillie to the theatre, the Derby Grand Theatre. As usual, she kept him waiting for her, and he said, laughing at her, ' "You would get me vexed, Lillie." but immediately afterwards added, "But no one can be vexed with you." ' (9) He took Lillie to see a sensational play which had played to great success in London the previous year, playing for over one hundred nights at the Princess's theatre, bemusing the critics and wowing the audiences. Called *The Still Alarm*, it was a set in a New York fire house (fire station), and was a stirring play which climaxed in a spectacular fire, with a special engine scene , and two live, twin Arabian horses, Bucephalus and Pegasus appearing on stage, also featuring a dog.

But even as they watched it, Robert and Lillie were planning a much more dramatic and sensational performance of their own.

The following day, a Saturday, Robert seemed to be preoccupied at work, and barely spoke to anyone. Work finished at midday, and he went back to his lodgings at Mr. Waterfall's house, 14 Stafford Street, and there the servant saw him put on his slippers and throw his hat into the corner before going to the window and sitting with his head on his arms. She said that for the last fortnight he had looked dull and gloomy, sitting with his head in his hands, 'whereas he used to be cheerful and have a smile on his face.' (2) On the day before, she observed, 'he looked very vexed.' (2) Later, he took a walk into town, to the Market Head shop of Messrs Dobson and Rosson, Gunsmiths. There he produced a small, nickel-plated revolver, known in the trade as a lady's revolver, and bought cartridges to fit it. The assistant told the authorities that the young man seemed in excellent spirits, and that 'he asked for the cartridges in a cool, gentlemanly manner, and there was nothing in his behaviour to excite the least fear…' (19)

Lillie was preparing in her own way for the coming tragedy. At three o'clock that afternoon, at home with Clara Williams, she told Clara that she was going to Nottingham that evening with Robert. Mrs. Williams brought up the subject of what she would like for Sunday's dinner, and Lillie said, ' "But I shan't want any if I die." ' (13) and Clara ignored it, being used to her morbid talk. Later, Lillie remarked to Clara, ' "How funny it would be if they were to find us dead in the railway carriage. Only we should miss the best of the fun, we should like to hear what they say when they open the carriage door." ' (13) She also said that ' "We are going to cause a great sensation tonight in Derby," ' (10) and that she ' regretted that she would not be able to hear the newsboys shouting the news of the occurrence, and witness the faces of the people who came to the door of the compartment.' (14) Mrs Williams said ' "You'd look well if it was to happen, or there was to be a collision and you should be killed." ' (13) Lillie laughed and said for Clara to take no notice of her, and indeed, Mrs. Williams had heard such seemingly wild statements so often before that she didn't.

*　*　*　*　*

Lillie took extra care in dressing for her trip to Nottingham, putting on clean linen and telling Mrs. Williams that if she was to die, she wanted to look her best. She said she was expecting a letter telling her what time train she and Robert were catching, and Mrs. Williams said she thought that the couple were planning to elope, and wanted her and her husband to believe something else, and Lillie laughed and said, "No fear!" (15)

Feron called for Lillie at five minutes to six that evening, in a hansom cab he had hired to take them to the station. Lillie was not fully dressed, and they stood talking on the stairs up to her room for a few minutes. Faron had a small bag in his hand, and he told her they were lilies, for her. He produced a spray of lilies of the valley and pinned them to the breast of her dress. Mrs Williams thought Faron was a little strange in his manner; he 'did not look her straight in the face,' (15) but Mrs Williams put it down to the fact that he had recently asked her to consider taking a house in the country with two rooms for Lillie, and had promised to pay her fifteen shillings (75p) weekly if she did. Mrs. Williams had refused because she thought Feron 'was not "quite right," and would come more frequently than was necessary.' (15) Robert told Lillie that the cab was waiting and went outside to wait for her. She came down and bid Mrs. Williams goodbye but not before asking her to leave the key in the window in case she came home late, then she left and drove to the railway station with her lover.

If they had been hoping for a compartment to theirselves they were to be disappointed. The 6.54pm express train was packed with people returning from Derby races. Reaching Nottingham at 7.27p.m., they got out and walked to the nearby Talbot Hotel, a lively place they had visited before, then around nine o'clock they made their way back to Nottingham railway station. The mail train from Lincoln to Tamworth steamed into Nottingham Midland Station at 9.10pm, and several people saw the young couple cross the footbridge to Platform 1, where the train stood. Witnesses spoke of them being in good spirits, 'talking and laughing together.' (4) Perhaps the grimmest occurrence, however, was

Trent Station, Nottingham,
where Robert and Lilly were discovered shot in a train compartment

reported in several papers from another witness:

'Before the return journey commenced, Feron also 'gaily remarked to an acquaintance on the Nottingham platform that he was about to commit suicide, but the remark was not taken seriously, as '...being accompanied by the girl it was thought that he jestingly referred to his approaching marriage.' (10)

The young couple found a compartment to themselves, next to the mail van. It was lit by a lantern, and the porter locked the compartment door before the train left the station. No one else got into the compartment with them, and nothing seemed out of order to him. It took six minutes to reach the next stop, Trent Station, at 9.31pm, and Amos Taylor, a porter-guard, unlocked the compartment and called out, "Tickets, please." He got no answer, then observed 'that there was a quantity of blood on the seats,' (9) and called the train's guard, a man called Hancock, and a colleague, foreman John Greene, who climbed into the compartment. He was met with a horrific scene.

* * * * *

Lillie Burford was sitting with her back to the engine in the far corner, leaning back with her head to the left, and blood was running down her left shoulder. Feron was on the opposite side, in the middle seat, with his head on the arm of the seat. Greene observed that Lillie was still alive, and thought that Feron was too, but that he died almost immediately that Greene got into the carriage. He then saw that Lillie had a wound in her temple, which was still bleeding, on the left side of her head. She was unconscious but breathing lightly. The *Sheffield Daily Telegraph* reported that she 'groaned unceasingly,' (3) but no other papers report it, nor was it mentioned at the inquest, so that can probably be taken as a journalist's invention.

As there was no doctor available at Trent Station, it was decided not to remove the couple, but to send the train on to Derby, and Amos Taylor and another porter, George Robinson travelled to Derby in the compartment with them. It must have been a gruesome journey of fifteen minutes or so for them, in a dimly lit railway carriage with a dead man and a dying woman, blood soaked into the seating and dripping onto the floor of the compartment.

While the train was travelling onward, John Greene sent a telegraph message from Trent Station to the Derby Station Master, Mr. Maxey, who notified a Detective Hole and Inspector J. Aldred.

Derby Railway Station where police waited to inspect the tragedy

It read, 'Two passengers are shot in the train. Have doctor ready.' (9) They sent out for medical assistance, 'the ambulance equipage was got ready,' (4) and when the train arrived at 9.48p.m., a Dr. Cassidi was waiting. The train pulled in by arrangement on platform three, close to the Ladies Room. Newspapers reported that 'The affair had been kept as quiet as possible, and there were not many people around at the time.' (9)

First the detectives entered the carriage and carefully examined the scene. Feron had fallen to one side, his head resting on his arm, as if asleep. Blood was oozing from a shot-wound in his right temple, and his light-coloured jacket was stained with blood, the carriage seat being also saturated with it. Burford was leaning on the arm rest in the corner opposite and blood was 'flowing freely from a similar wound in her left temple' (4) and down over the shoulder of a macintosh she was wearing. She was still breathing and was removed and sent by ambulance to the Derbyshire Royal Infirmary not far away at the end of Midland Road. Feron was quite clearly dead, and his body was taken by cab to the mortuary at the Infirmary. When his body was lifted, a revolver was revealed, with two chambers having been discharged. More cartridges were later found in Feron's vest pocket. Seven letters were also found on the seat, one a love letter to Feron from Lillie, the others were written in French by Feron and had blood upon

Derby Royal Infirmary, where the bodies were brought, and the inquest held

them. A Police Constable Ashton searched Feron's body and found only four shillings and elevenpence-halfpenny (approximately 25p), keys, an ABC timetable, handkerchief, and six bullets already mentioned. He also found a flattened bullet on the seat next to Burford's body, a woman's slipper and a pair of men's gloves. Nothing of importance was found upon Lillie. It's a chilling side note that no first-class railway tickets were found, further evidence of intent to commit suicide before the journey reached its end.

*   *   *   *   *

Lillie died within fifteen minutes of being brought into the Infirmary, and her body was removed to the mortuary, where she was laid upon a slab close by the body of her lover.

Somehow the girl's identity was discovered, and her address, presumably from her letter to Feron, and Clara Williams and her husband were informed that night by Station Master Maxey who knocked on their door shortly before eleven. Remembering Lillie's jokes about dying with Feron, the Williams's searched her room to see if she had left a note that explained her reasons. There, under her pillow, they discovered two letters from the real George in Kidsgrove to Lilley, one enclosing ten shillings (50p), money to support his child by her, and saying, 'Dear Lil, I enclose 10 shillings, hope you will write better another time, as yours was not at all ladylike, George.' (15) Mr. Williams spoke to the newpapers rather bitterly of the petty ruse played by Lillie on the Williams's hospitality in passing Robert off as her fiancé. He disclosed that Lillie had always called Robert by the name of George in front of them, saying, ' "Our suspicions were not aroused until we found a letter from her lover under her pillow. Of course, we then knew that the deceased (Feron) was not the person she told us he was. The deception was all carried out by the girl." ' (10)

*   *   *   *   *

A preliminary inquest was held at the Infirmary on the Monday morning, by Coroner Close. Lillie was formally identified by her mother, Elizabeth Burford. She was terribly distressed and immediately she caught sight of Lillie's form, she cried out, "Oh, my poor Lillie, my beautiful girl," (9) and fainted. Robert Feron's workmate and friend, a Mr. Jean Baptiste Kalthmont D'Aubry, was similarly moved to see his dead companion, and kissed Robert's cheek whilst 'crying bitterly.' (7) Identification then having been made, the coroner adjourned the inquest until Wednesday to enable further details to be gathered.

The inquest was resumed on Wednesday at the Guildhall, when the Coroner was satisfied that he had enough evidence to lay before the jury to enable them to reach a proper conclusion in the case. It had also given time for Feron's uncle and a cousin to travel over from Belgium, though they did not speak at the inquest, nor did they give any newspaper interviews, indeed, they are barely mentioned and not described at all. They seem to have come to settle up any debts left behind by Robert, and to take his body home as quietly and unobtrusively as possible.

The first part of the inquest was an inquiry into the death of Lillie. Lillie's mother gave evidence first. She stated that Lillie had come to Derby a fortnight ago the previous Thursday, which is really astounding, if one reflects that that gave Lillie and Robert only fifteen days in which to meet, become lovers and plot their deaths together! Elizabeth Burford said that her daughter 'had tried dressmaking and that did not suit her, and she then took it into her head to be an actress.' (16)

One can sense a certain disapproval of her daughter in those phrases 'did not suit her' and 'took it into her head', so that it is left to speculate if Lillie's leaving Spennymoor and coming to Derby was because of some family disagreement, or perhaps because of an ultimatum that now Lilllie's child was six months old and probably weaned she had to get a job. Her father was a watchman at a local ironworks, not a highly paid job; money must have been tight. Or was it that Lillie just wasn't cut out for the drudgery of motherhood, for humdrum work in a milliner's, and the gritty life of a Northern town? When asked if she had any communication with her daughter since she had left Spennymoor, Elizabeth said she had one letter, written the previous week and received last Thursday. Lillie said in it that she had been very ill on Sunday and, melodramatically, 'did not believe she could live over Sunday night.' (13) She then said that 'if she got better,' she would look for a job. Asked by the Coroner if she still had the letter, Elizabeth said she had burnt it. One wonders if she burnt it out of frustration with her daughter, or if there was more in the letter which reflected badly on Lillie and she did not want it known. It all seems a little strange, like an unplanned or unexplained departure, for Elizabeth Burford said that at first she thought her daughter had gone to Oldham, until she received a letter. Oldham was where Lillie had begun her acting career; perhaps she still had stage friends there.

Lillie's life seems strange. She did not like the idea of being a milliner but couldn't break into the theatrical world she so adored. Her downfall was her vanity. She was a beautiful young woman who was 'fond of company and admiration,' (16) but she had no talent for the theatre, where she had envisioned herself performing centre stage, being admired and adored, like so many other stars of the Victorian stage and music-hall. The *Newcastle Daily Journal*, drawing on local interviews, put it succinctly:

'She was described as an actress, but whilst she had figured in pantomime, her education was not sufficient to entitle her to take a leading part. She had a strong desire to take this position at the footlights, but there the tendency of her ambition ended.' (16)

Basically, poor Lillie had no talent, and she had failed to make the grade. The world she so loved, of lights and music and applause, had rejected her. What was there in life for her? she must have reasoned to herself. Nothing but drudgery in a lowly-paid job – if she could get work at all.

A letter was shown at the inquest, then, to her mother. It was one of the letters found in the carriage after Lillie's and Robert's deaths. It was addressed to a childhood friend of Lillie's, back in Spennymoor, a young woman called Minny Whitehead, in Lillie's hometown of Spennymoor. It makes plain her desire to end her life:

'Darling Minnie – You will think it strange to receive a letter from me so soon after the other one, but darling I am tired of my life. I can't always be with him I love, so have come to the conclusion it will be better to die with him. Goodbye darling and think of me sometimes. Darling Lily.' (2)

Lillie's mother denied that the letter was in Lillie's handwriting, although admitting that she could write in several different hands, and flatly denied that Lillie would ever kill herself, but that refusal to face the evidence seems on a par with others who knew Lillie back in Spennymoor, denying that she could ever envisage it, giving such reasons as '…far too fond of life…', '(not) capable of thinking of such a thing.' (1) It was a hard thing for those she left behind to accept, but given that Lillie had already told Clara Williams where, when and how she intended to die, there seems no doubt that she was a willing partner in the suicide pact. Perhaps what really upset Lillie's mother and made it hard for her to admit Lillie had willingly made such a suicide pact was that there was no farewell letter from Lillie to her, nor any mention of the baby of six months, her young son, she was abandoning without any seeming regret. Lillie seems to have been very self-centred.

Clara Williams gave evidence next and left no one in any doubt that Lillie was capable of suicide and had planned to die with her lover. She repeated what Lillie had said about dying with Robert Feron, to seeing Feron with a revolver, and of Lillie leaving with him on Saturday, predicting beforehand to Clara what would happen on the train from Nottingham.

Clara was followed by Alexander Taylor, a post office clerk, who saw the young couple cross the footbridge onto the platform and enter the train alone. No one else entered the compartment before the train drew out, and the obvious implication was that Feron and Lillie had not been killed by someone else. He heard no gunshots whilst travelling in the mail carriage next to their compartment.

Amos Taylor, porter at Trent Station, was acting as ticket collector and spoke to finding the couple, shot in the carriage, when he unlocked the door. He and George Robinson travelled on to Derby with the couple. He observed that the young lady was breathing and thought that Feron breathed, and saw his foot move when he first entered the compartment to examine Lillie and Robert, but said he was dead when the train reached Derby.

Charles Hole, Detective Inspector in the employ of the Midland Railway, then gave evidence as to what he found when he searched the compartment, which brought the letters into evidence. Apart from the letter to Lillie's friend Milly and one to Robert's employer, Mr. Holme, they were written in French, and Feron's friend, workmate and Spanish tutor, Mr. D'Aubray, was called upon to translate aloud to the Coroner's court. The first letter, to Robert's friend, Fritz Patte, in Brussels, explains a lot:

'My dear Fritz, I am going to be buried in the earth without shaking hands with you for the last time. I have had no luck, because you know what I had before going to Brussels. I will never get over it. I have already spent more than 400 francs at the doctor's, but I don't get much better. You will be the only one in Brussels who knows my secret…' (2)

This is quite a clear admission to his friend that he has contracted some sort of venereal disease, most probably syphilis, which was incurable in his day, and was a rampant disease in Victorian times. Treatment, as Robert was finding, was expensive, and only partially relieved the suffering. A long drawn-out, painful disease that wasted both body and mind, and the shame it would cause his family back home, were obviously too much for Feron to contemplate enduring, and so he decided to end it all. As the writer Julian Barnes said on the subject, in an article on the appalling suffering of the French writer Daudet, who contracted syphilis in the late 1800's and which perfectly captures Feron's reasoning and conclusion: '…the anticipation of indignities to come – and the terror of disgusting those you love – makes suicide not just tempting but logical.' (17)

*   *   *   *   *

We see now what the papers were plainly saying to their readers when they said that 'he had been leading a gay life,' (7) for in Victorian times 'gay' was not shorthand for homosexuality, but meant that the 'gay' person was sexually promiscuous, usually heterosexually. We see, too, perhaps why Mr. Holme wrote to Brussels some months previously saying that Robert had got beyond his control. He was sent abroad too young, with too little supervision and too much money. Small wonder he came to grief. As an acquaintance said to one newspaper, 'women have been his ruin.' (11)

Feron went on in his letter to say that Fritz was the only one in Brussels who knew his secret, that Feron could not bring himself to tell his father what illness he had, that 'I simply tell him that I have something frightful.' (2) He told Fritz that, besides, he was over 1,000 francs in debt, and that he intended to kill himself. He wrote that also that he loved an actress who loved him, and that she was not afraid to die and 'will kill herself with me.' (2) He said that he 'would' do it in a railway carriage,' and intimated that he would probably have to complete the act for Lillie as she 'might be weak and feeble at the last moment.' (2) He asked to be remembered sometimes and asked his friend to give his kisses to Fritz's mother and brother.

The next letter Mr. D'Aubrey read out (crying the while), was to Robert's mother. Robert said that he didn't want her to think that he 'was sad to die, as 'life had become fearful' to him. He told her that he was 'condemned', and 'I cannot live much longer, therefore I think that it will be better to have done with it all at once.' (2) He had been home at New Year and his mother had said how ill he had looked. He told her that she had been right, that 'I really was half dead, and it took me all my time to look cheerful. It was because I was suffering so much. Every morning I required all my energy to enable me to rise. My stay in England has been fatal.' (2) Further, he begged his mother not to send his younger brother, Ernest, to England in case the same thing happened to him, 'as there are the same dangers for him as for me. You do not know all the opportunities I had here.' He said, 'My stay in England has been fatal,' and that, 'You know a young man here has too much liberty and takes advantage of it.' (2) He told his mother that he intended dying with a young girl, an actress, who loved him passionately, and that 'She also is going to kill herself,' (2) and said that he must be buried with her if they did die together, otherwise he wished his body to be taken back to Brussels, then a phrase that must have suffered slightly in translation: 'It is so far, I won't wait any longer.' (2) Presumably Robert meant the disease he suffered had developed (so far gone) to a stage where he had to take action while he was still able to function independently. He sent love and kisses to all the family and said how sad it was he couldn't kiss his mother and father one last time, then signed off with 'but you know I cannot live any longer.' (2)

To his father, Robert wrote begging forgiveness for what he was about to do. He told him: 'I prefer not to tell you the reason of my suicide, because it is the word. It is a very terrible reason, my father, and I would never have been happy because I am convinced there is no means to get out of it.' (2) Again he repeats his warning not to send his brother Ernest to England, saying that his father would regret it, and pitifully says, 'You know I was not a bad boy, and you see what has happened.' (2) He asks his father to please settle his debts in Derby, which he has detailed in a separate letter to Mr. D'Aubry, asking him to take the payments for him. It would have been interesting to know whom he owed in Derby, and what for. Then he closes by asking for forgiveness and one last kiss.

To a cousin called George he confided in another letter, in case there was any doubt that Lillie was a willing conspirator, and not an unsuspecting victim, as some friends claimed, the details of what seems a well-planned pact: 'We are going by rail to Nottingham… We will enjoy ourselves during the evening. Then we will take the train to come back and I will shoot my mistress in the temple. Then, I will kill myself afterwards. She wants me to do it in this manner as she cannot handle a revolver.' (2)

Robert also wrote to Mr. Holme, his employer, thanking him for his kindness and apologising for the trouble he had caused him, sending his love to Mr. Holme's family and saying, quite truthfully, 'I know I should have been better, but I am so young, and there was no one to look after me.' (2) To Mr. D'Aubry, he sent a a statement of his debts and asked his friend to settle them for him, saying Robert's father would send him a cheque for 34 pounds, which would include cab fare, as Robert didn't want Mr. D'Aubry to walk. He again refers to his illness by saying, 'Do not believe that I am sorry to die. I assure you it affords me an immense pleasure for … I feel that I would never get over that confounded illness.' (2)

The reading of the letters caused a great sensation in the court, and all the women present were said to have been openly weeping as well as poor Mr. D'Aubry, who had so recently kissed the cheek of his dead friend. D'Aubry sat down, and Detective Inspector Hole gave evidence as to finding the revolver with two chambers discharged, and also a spent bullet, lying loose on the middle seat of the compartment, opposite Feron's body.

Mr. John Acton Southern, who was house surgeon at the Royal Infirmary, gave evidence then on his examination of Lillie's body.

He testified that:

'…Burford was taken to the Infirmary at about 10 o'clock on Saturday. She was unconscious and remained so up till death, which took place fifteen minutes after admission. There was a wound on the left temple and the skin around it was blackened. There was a strong smell of burnt gunpowder. He had since made a postmortem examination and found a small aperture in the left temple. There was considerable destruction of the brain and the right side of the skull was fractured. Close to the fracture he found a bullet, and the cause of death he attributed to the injury to the brain, which would in all probability have been caused by a shot from a revolver. The bullet ran in a backward direction across the skull and he was of the opinion that the wound was not self-inflicted because it was on the left side of the head.' (2)

Here the coroner interrupted to ask Elizabeth Burford if her daughter had been left-handed and was told she was not.

The doctor finished by saying that the positions the two people had been found in were consistent with Feron firing into Lillie's head from where he was sitting.

The Coroner then briefly summed up in the case of Lillie Burford's death. He said the jury had to consider by what means she met her death and thought that from the evidence of the doctor they would have no doubt that it was by a shot from a revolver. If they reached that belief, then the question arose as to how, and by what means and by whom that wound was caused. Mr. Coles then drew particular attention to one of Feron's letters in which he said that he would shoot his mistress in the temple and then shoot himself. He asked the jury if it was possible that Burford had 'committed the rash act,' (2) but if they believed the evidence before them, they could do no other than find Feron guilty of wilful murder. Within fifteen minutes the jury were back with their verdict: wilful murder against the deceased, Robert Feron.

The second inquest, on Robert Feron, then began. The Coroner said that the jury would have to take into consideration the cause of Feron's death and the state of his mind when the act was committed.

Evidence was again given as to the finding of the bodies, and then Dr. Southern testified as to the postmortem he conducted on

POLICE *THE ILLUSTRATED* NEWS

LAW COURTS AND WEEKLY RECORD

No. 1,315.   SATURDAY, APRIL 27, 1889.   Price One Penny.

THE MURDER & SUICIDE IN A RAILWAY CARRIAGE

How the Police News pictured the Derby Tragedy

Feron. He said that there was a wound in each temple, that the bullet had entered at the right temple and exited through the left temple. The position of the wound and the marks were such as to lead him to the belief that the fatal wound was self-inflicted.

This would explain the loose bullet on the middle seat, by Lillie. Robert would have turned away slightly from her and shot himself, and the bullet, more or less spent, would have dropped or rebounded lightly, onto the seat beside her.

Mr. D'Aubrey then gave evidence. He said he had known Feron for eighteen months, since Robert first came to England. He had assisted Mr. D'Aubrey in his work conducting commercial foreign correspondence for Mr. Holme, and though he wasn't paid, he 'had plenty of money, sent to him by his father,' and 'deceased never complained about not having sufficient money, but spent it very freely.' (2) He spoke also of Feron's last few days. The young Belgian had been off work since Wednesday, and on Thursday he visited him and found him very low. He said he had a cold and a headache. D'Aubrey said that he told him to stay at home and keep warm. He observed that deceased had often seemed depressed and ill lately, and he had told him not to stay out late at night. When Robert had come into work, on Saturday, he had barely spoken all morning. He said that in sorting out Feron's effects at his lodgings after Robert's death, he had come across a Belgian newspaper with a detailed, long account of the recent suicide of the Crown Prince of Austria, and that 'the deceased seemed to have studied this.' (2)

Thirty-year-old Crown Prince Rudolf, heir to the Austro-Hungarian Empire, had killed himself in a suicide pact with his seventeen-year-old mistress Baroness Maria Vetsera at his hunting lodge only three months before, in late January of 1889, and it had been a huge sensation across Europe. His father, Emperor Franz Joseph, had refused Rudolf permission to divorce his wife and marry the Baroness Maria. Like Robert, Rudolf, had shot himself and his mistress. Ironically, the reason for the suicide is believed to have been in part because Rudolf also had an incurable venereal disease, though this was not publicised at the time, and some historians suggest that he was haunted with guilt for infecting his wife. Whatever, it seems to have rung a chime with Robert Feron, and he must have seen his own death as attracting some of the glamour and attention the sad deaths at Mayerling had been given by the world's press.

Emily Smith, servant to Mr. Waterfall, with whom Robert Feron lodged at 14 Stafford Street, told the inquest that for the last fortnight of his life the deceased had been gloomy and looked ill. He often sat with his head in his hands, whereas before he had used to be smiling and cheerful. On the day of his death he had come home from work, put his slippers on and thrown his hat into the corner of the room and put his coat on the sofa. He then went to the window where he sat with his head on his arms. Witness said this 'was altogether different to his usual custom, and on the day before, the Friday, he had looked very vexed.' (2) He was also only eating half of what he used to eat.

Mr. Thomas Cartwright, head book-keeper to Mr. Holme, said that he had known Feron for eighteen months, and he 'had always been remarkable for his cheerfulness and amiability.' (2) After Robert had not come to work on Thursday, he called upon him and found him 'in a very depressed condition; in fact, he had never seen him in such a condition before.' (2)

This was all the evidence called by the Coroner, and he told the jury that there was no doubt as to the cause of death, but 'the question was with regard to the state of the deceased's mind at the time. To his mind it was perfectly clear, and, taking all the circumstances into consideration, he thought this would be the only verdict they could arrive at.' (2) Thus directed by the coroner, the jury returned a verdict of 'Suicide whilst in a state of unsound mind.' (2)

This must have been a relief to the Feron family, and the silent onlookers at the inquest, Robert's uncle and cousin, both unnamed. If the jury had brought in a different verdict applicable at the time, that of 'felo de se' (literally "evildoer against oneself"), Robert's body could not have been released to the family, but 'would have been interred between the hours of nine and twelve o'clock at night, and within twelve hours of the finding of the verdict.' (2)

Despite Robert wishing to be buried with his lover, it was not to be. Plans had been made, and his body 'was placed in an elm shell enclosed in a lead coffin, with polished oak outer coffin mounted with brass furniture. It was made by Mr. Jones, of the Market-place, Derby, and the plate bore the following inscription: "Robert Feron, born 7th October 1870, died 13th April 1889." ' (2) As Robert had been a suicide, a special release order had to be given by the Deputy Mayor for his body to be taken out of the borough, and his remains were taken to the Midland Station, accompanied by one of Mr. Jones' (the undertaker) men, where it was transported to

Harwich, 'where they were placed in the care of a gentleman from Brussels, who will take them… to Brussels.' (2) Robert's uncle and cousin left Derby on the same train.

The whole affair briefly known as 'The Derby Tragedy' was summed up by a Victorian magazine and served as the epitaph for both Robert and Lillie:

'The Derby Tragedy is the outcome of the youthful pessimism of the age and the mad seeking for advertisement. The poor girl left it on record that she wished she could have seen the fuss that would be made about her. It is all very sad, but it is less a sign of the times, and carries its own moral.' (18)

Lillie's funeral took place on the Thursday 18th April 1889, in the New Cemetery, Derby. It was sparsely attended, no prior notice being given, and there were only eight mourners at the graveside. Naive, vain Lillie would have been terribly disappointed. Her 'great sensation' had lasted six days. The pathetic dream-damaged children were buried apart from each other, and the world moved on with its business.

REFERENCES

1. *Durham County Advertiser*, Friday 29th April 1889.
2. *Derby Mercury*, Wednesday 24th April 1889.
3. *Sheffield Daily Telegraph*, Monday 15th April 1889.
4. *Derby Daily Telegraph*, Monday 15th April 1889.
5. *Lloyd's Weekly London Newspaper*, Sunday 21st April 1889.
6. *Derby Daily Telegraph*, Thursday 18th April 1889.
7. *Alnwick & County Gazette*, Saturday 20th April 1889.
8. *Nottingham Evening Post*, Thursday 18th April 1889.
9. *Derby Mercury*, Wednesday 17th April 1889.
10. *Nottingham Evening Post*, Monday 15th April 1889.
11. *Sheffield and Rotherham Independent*, Tuesday 16th April 1889.
12. *Illustrated Police News*, Saturday 27th April 1889.
13. *The Derbyshire Courier*, Saturday 20th April 1889.
14. *The London Daily News*, Tuesday 16th April 1889.
15. *Sheffield and Rotherham Independent*, Thursday 18th April 1889.
16. *Newcastle Daily Journal*, Thursday 18th April 1889.
17. *The Art of Suffering* by Julian Barnes,
        The Guardian, Saturday 11th May 2002.
18. *The Referee*, Sunday 21st April 1889.
19. *The Leicester Daily Post*, 17th April 1889.

'WHERE'S THE BODY?' – THE BRADWELL MYSTERY
MARTHA BUTTERY / BUTTRESS, BRADWELL 30TH APRIL 1885

Visitors to the Peak District travelling between Tideswell with its beautiful church 'The Cathedral of the Peak', and Castleton with its show-caves and Blue John shops, usually pass through without stopping to look at the little village of Bradwell, and miss its charm, as it is a village that has been built with its back to the road. To really see the place, one must leave the car and walk its ancient lanes and footpaths that wind around the hillside it is built upon before appreciating its strange charm. Seth Evans, who recorded the history of the place wrote in 1912:

'Its steep winding streets – if streets they can be called – and all sorts of queer little out of the way places running in and out in all directions, break neck, oblique, skew-tilted, beginning everywhere, leading nowhere, make the stranger feel that he is living in medieval times. Occupied by the Romans, who left their traces everywhere… this romantic spot was never troubled with a surveyor. Every man was his own architect. He built what he liked where he liked, and as he liked, with the result that in the twentieth century there remains one of the most comical looking, beautiful and picturesque old towns ever in picturesque Peakland.' (1)

But, for lovers of the macabre, there is an added attraction which seems ideal for this setting, and it is to be found in the graveyard of Bradwell's church of St. Barnabas. To stand in the small, open space of turf close to the church porch, between the shared grave of Joseph and Fanny Townsend and the grave of Florence Bradwell, is

John Buttery's unmarked grave is the patch between other graves

to stand at the heart of one of the grimmest and yet most fascinating tales of the Peak. It is here, in Plot 190 on the sexton's plan of the graveyard that the answer to what the newspapers of the time called 'The Bradwell Mystery' lies buried in an unmarked grave, and since that hot sunny day in June of 1885, no new evidence has come to light to show whether the man who is buried here was in fact a murderer, or a wronged and innocent party, hounded by wagging tongues to an early grave.

Examining the sexton's map, however, leads us to ask two very interesting questions.

The first question to ask is, why is there no headstone or grave-surround to show that someone lies buried here? It is not, comparatively, an old grave; older graves nearby have kept all their funereal masonry, so it becomes clear that no one erected a stone ever to inform future generations of the dead person's identity. Only the sexton's map shows us that the burial space is occupied, and that an 'M.J. Buttery' lies below.

Looking at the map closely, we can read in the faded, sepia

copperplate script that this M.J. Buttery was buried at a depth of seven feet, which leads us to the second question: why should this be, when six feet is the accepted depth for a single burial?

Let us examine what is known, and conjecture from these facts the answers to the two questions.

The man who was buried in this grave was known, although his real name was Matthew James Buttery, as James Buttress to the people of Bradwell. There is little difference between the two surnames, and if one tries saying 'Buttery's house', for example, in a Derbyshire accent, then the name does come out as 'Buttress'. This last name is the one most used in the newspaper accounts of 'The Bradwell Mystery', and on occasions when newspapers are read, the reader should be aware that Buttress and Buttery were the same man.

Well over a hundred years have passed now, and those who knew Buttery had their own reasons for wanting him to be forgotten by the world, so we have little evidence to tell us what kind of man he was. There are no portraits or early photographs, no memoirs or published recollections of anyone in, or close to, the Buttery family. However, if we take the evidence given at the inquest and what old newspapers tell us and put it to the background knowledge gained through further research, it is possible to build up a profile of the man.

We are told that he was a large man, strong and powerfully built. This was the result of a lifetime's hard work as a labourer, stone-mason and drystone waller, for though he and his wife Martha owned a small farm in Bradwell, it was only two fields and a couple of cows, not enough to support them entirely, and Buttery needed money frequently, for he was a heavy drinker. In temperament, though most people found him to be 'harmless and inoffensive', (2) as a policeman later testified, he could be moody and violent, taking his rages out on his wife, of whom he was insanely jealous.

Buttery was a native of Alport, in the nearby Woodlands Valley, which winds up from the north-western tip of Ladybower Reservoir and extends as far as the Snake Inn on the Snake Pass. Before the dams were built this was a remote and sparsely populated area, and as late as the eighteenth century, local tradition maintained, the men living here and in the adjoining Derwent Valley were feared, and regarded as 'savages', raiding settlements beyond Bamford, and carrying off the womenfolk. Perhaps there was in Buttery some of this wild savageness still lurking, something which 'came out in the blood'.

Of Buttery's childhood we know little except that he was one of at least eight children, and that his father was also a farmer in a small way. When James was eight years old, His sister Anne married a Bradwell man, William Bramall, whose family farmed and kept the Bowling Green Tavern at Smalldale, a hamlet on the edge of Bradwell which was slowly being absorbed into the village proper. From this marriage probably dates James's visits to the village, and the bond between the two families was further strengthened when in 1885 another of James's sisters, Nancy, married William Bramall's brother Joseph, and also went to live at the Bowling Green Tavern.

From the earliest of times Bradwell had been a leadmining community. Local tales have it that the folk of the village were descended from slaves brought in by the Romans to work their mines, and some historians in the nineteenth century noted that the Bradwell people, who were notoriously clannish in those days, insular and distrustful of strangers, seemed markedly different in their physical appearance from other residents of the Peak District, being squat and dark of countenance. Inter-marriage was the custom, and young men who attempted to marry 'out of the village' were often prevented from doing so by family or friends, having to 'encounter the collective vengeance of the ladies both old and young', (1) as one writer recorded. Any young man who came courting was speedily seen off by the youths of the village, or had to pay a tax called 'footling ale', the fine being one shilling and sevenpence (7p), and 'if the interloper would not pay, a halter was put round his neck, and he was driven round the village,' (1) as one historian recorded in 1901.

The insularity of the folk of the Hope Valley is well caught in a local proverb, which goes: 'Mony a one lives in Hope (the next village to Bradwell), as never saw Castleton.' It's worth noting for those who do not know the area that Castleton is only a mile from Hope! This insularity is stressed since, as will be seen later, it has a direct relevance to the case, and may be one of the strongest arguments against Buttery's proclaimed innocence.

Whatever the native's distrust of interlopers, James Buttery seems to have been accepted by the people of Bradwell, for in his early manhood he was living at Smalldale and courting a woman he must have known since he was a child, as she only lived a hundred yards or so up the lane from the Bowling Green Tavern. On February 15th, 1860, it was recorded in the parish register at Hope Church (Bradwell church not having yet been built) that James Buttery, 22, bachelor of Smalldale, married Martha Wright, 35, spinster, of Smalldale.

By all accounts Martha was a striking-looking woman when she was young and this – and the fact that she brought money to the marriage – most probably accounts for the fact that James was prepared to marry a woman some thirteen years his senior. It may have been that they were forced by parental opposition to delay marrying. James was twenty-two, a year past the age of majority and living away from home, so his parents could not have stopped it, but Martha's widowed mother only died the month before the wedding, and within six weeks of burying the old lady they were married, scant time for mourning. It is also known that Martha and her brother, Joseph, were very 'close' with their money, and this frugality came from their mother, who had been widowed some nineteen years earlier and struggled to raise the children and run a small farm with their aid. Perhaps old lady Wright was against her daughter marrying a penniless young man like Buttery and was unwilling to settle a dowry on her daughter – and also lose her help on the farm.

Or was there another reason for her opposition to the marriage: did she see in James Buttery some of the 'dissolute habits and violent temper' (2) which were to make her daughter so unhappy in later years? Did she, sensibly, oppose the marriage while ever she lived?

Whatever, with the death of their mother, Joseph Wright kept the farm and settled a sum of money on his sister Martha as part of the inheritance, though how much is disputed. Some gossips later claimed that it was a thousand pounds, along with some property, while others put it at only three hundred, still a good sum in those times. It is known that the newly-weds were able to settle in a house of 'rather more substantial erection than the rest of the scattered dwellings which constitute Smalldale… and enjoyed the importance which always attaches to moneyed people in country places.' (3)

For some years the couple lived amicably together. In early 1862 Martha gave birth to their first child, a girl named Elizabeth, followed in December of the same year by a son, James William, but he lived for only six weeks. Two more children were born, Martha in 1864, and Nancy in 1866, but there was to be no son and heir, and this may have added to James's moroseness and sudden outbursts of violent temper. In the mid-1870's he began to drink heavily, and grew violently jealous of Martha, accusing her of infidelity and beating her on occasion. Neighbours later said that 'it was no uncommon thing for them to be aroused from their sleep by screams and cries of "murder!" from Mrs. Buttery.' (3)

For her part, Martha was known in the village as being ' possessed of a rather uncertain temper', and with a 'tongue that outran her discretion.' (3) As the money dwindled, all finally being lost on a disastrous speculation on a carting business, her nearness with money would cause her to berate her drunken husband. It was an ever-tightening screw of circumstances that would lead to tragedy, for the less money they had, the more James drank, the more he drank the more he beat her, and the more he beat her, the more she took refuge away from the marital home, fuelling the accusations of infidelity he made against her. On several occasions Martha threatened to leave James, but it is significant in the light of later events that she only left home for a few days at a time when things were really bad, and then did not leave the village, staying at her sister's house not far away.

The couple seemed locked into a pattern of violence which increased as the years wore on, for Martha refused any outside help beyond the occasional days of refuge, and 'over and over again,' one newspaper correspondent learned, 'they made up their quarrels, and the woman has been known after such reconciliation to take her husband's part when his conduct has been condemned.' (3)

Something bound Martha to her husband: pride, love, a sense of duty, conventional expectations of behaviour, it is impossible to say what at this distance in time, but she suffered much at his hands and yet chose to stay. As she grew older, Martha began to show the strain of living with such a brute. Approaching her sixties, she grew thin and worn and suffered a slight stroke.

Far from mellowing towards his wife as she declined, James's behaviour grew much worse. Although some said he was drinking less, his attacks on Martha grew more frequent. By the early 1880's their three daughters had all left home to work in domestic service away from Bradwell, and so Martha had no one who could intervene on her behalf. In the opening months of 1885, two events occurred which should have warned Martha that it was definitely time to leave her husband while she was still able.

James and Martha owned two cows which they kept in a cowhouse or shippon in a field some distance behind their house. One night, Buttery ordered his wife to go to the shippon, saying that he would follow shortly. Something in his manner alerted Martha to danger, and when she left the house she went instead to the home of a relative, where she spent the night in safety. When she returned the next day James asked her why she did not go to the shippon as he'd ordered her to, and she told him that she was afraid that he was going to kill her there. James coldly told Martha that she was correct, 'as he had laid the plot beforehand.' (3) As if that was not warning enough, soon afterwards Buttery made a desperate attempt to take the life of his wife by hanging, though it isn't reported how she managed to escape with her life on that occasion.

In March 1885 things had become so bad that Martha went to the village policeman, P.C. Thomas Brown, showed him a black eye Buttery had given her, and asked for protection. Brown already knew of the couple's stormy marriage, since James had been to him on several occasions with tales that Martha was unfaithful and asked the policeman to keep watch on the Buttery house so that she could be caught in adultery. P.C. Brown refused to believe the allegations and would do nothing. The black eye was a different matter, however. Martha decided to press charges against her husband, and the constable must have taken some action, for later on he produced a document which James had written in his presence at that time. It read:

'Mr. Brown, Bradwell. Sir – we have made all things right now, so you must settle it and not let it go any further, for we have both agreed to be good with each other for twelve months and then we shall be good forrad (going forward, i.e. in future).' (2)

The promise did not last long, however, for by the end of April the couple were once more at odds with each other, and with a dreadful irony, their last argument was over a funeral.

A neighbour, an old leadminer called George Bradwell, had died, and Martha intended to go to his funeral at the Wesleyan chapel. For some reason James opposed this, but Martha went anyway, 'contrary to the wishes and threats of her husband'. (2) The exact nature of the threats he made is not known, but may be guessed at from the testimony of another mourner at the funeral who later informed the correspondent of a newspaper that Martha had told her that 'she was afraid her husband would murder her, as he got worse every day.' (2) Neighbours also testified that on the day of the funeral 'there were several quarrels of a violent nature.' (2)

On the following day, April 30th, Martha was seen by two people. One saw her early on in the day, cleaning her doorstep, and then, ominously in the light of later evidence, a neighbour saw her in the late afternoon, walking with James over the fields towards the shippon, presumably to milk the cows. From that time on, no one in Bradwell ever saw Martha again.

*　*　*　*　*

For a month Buttery told anyone who asked about Martha that his wife had left him. Although he appears to have made token enquiries amongst her relatives in the village, his neighbours soon began to suspect something. They later said that it was noticeable that on previous occasions when Martha had left home, James had attempted to find her and persuade her to return home, whereas this time he did not seem unduly concerned to trace her. To anyone who enquired further, James said that he believed Martha was staying in Manchester with one of their daughters, as she had threatened to do so before. This was accepted at first, as Martha was known to be very close to her children, but as a newspaper later reported: 'When a week and a fortnight had elapsed and it

Buttery's House at the time of the murder

was found that she was not with her relatives, the people became suspicious, and rumours of foul play got about.' (6) The most popular rumour was that Buttery had killed Martha and concealed her body inside their house.

To add to these rumours, James's behaviour became markedly strange also. His brother, who visited him from Sheffield, a fortnight after Martha's disappearance, said that James was in a 'very low way.' (2) A neighbour who called at the house frequently, most probably his brother-in-law, William Bramall, noted that he did not appear to be sleeping upstairs, but on the sofa in the living room instead. Indeed, James seemed to be having difficulty in sleeping at all, for he was 'very early astir' (2) and some mornings was seen returning from the milking in the shippon by five o'clock. Added to this, people met him out walking late at night, heading towards some mill dams at nearby Brough, 'carrying a bag and contents.' (2) The grisly inference of this rumour was left to each gossip's imagination.

In a small village of the nineteenth century, with little to relieve the tedium of everyday life, such talk must have been rife, and it was not helped when Buttery, who was always his own worst enemy, added to the gossip. One night when he was drunk, he confided to another man that it was his belief that Martha was 'no more than a mile away from here.' (3) Given that everyone knew by now that Martha was not staying with any friends or relatives in the village, there could only be one interpretation placed on that statement. Then there was James's dream, which he was rash enough to tell someone of, one night when he was drunk.

High on nearby Gawtrey Hill stood the Cronstadt Mine, its disused shaft plunging to a depth of 240 feet (over 73 metres). Foolishly, James confided that he had dreamed one night of Martha and the shaft, and this further added to the general suspicion of James. But still people hung back from directly confronting Buttery, from asking the awful question of him. No one seemed to think it their place to do so.

Action was finally taken on May 26th, when the three daughters, who had been told of their mother's disappearance, decided to put the matter in the hands of the local police, and someone acting on their behalf informed the village 'bobby', Constable Brown (who was probably already aware). Given at that time that there was no telephone system, and that the daughters were living as far apart from each other as Brighton, Manchester and Alrewas, Staffordshire, then it is perhaps understandable why it took them a month to act, but it didn't help the inquiry. If James had killed Martha, as people in the village were now openly saying, then he had had a lot of time to cover his tracks and conceal Martha's body. Murder investigators today acknowledge that the first forty-eight hours after a murder are the most vital, and the chances of a successful outcome to an investigation decrease in proportion to the time lost before detectives are called in.

That night Buttery received a visit from the vicar of Bradwell, the Reverend Dudley, 'in consequence of the distress of the daughters, who were anxious about their missing mother.' (2) One of the daughters, Nancy, was in service to the previous vicar of Bradwell, the Revd. Webb, now at Alrewas, and she was most likely the one who started the inquiries. The vicar of Hope village nearby, the Revd. Buckstone, had also been over to see Buttery with the same purpose, to see if Buttery could shed any light on the disappearance of his wife.

To Revd. Dudley, Buttery told the tale he had already told to others, with a few embellishments: Martha had gone; she had been unfaithful to him; she had taken with her £212. Again and again, Revd Dudley later testified, Buttery repeated the allegations of his wife's infidelity, and though the vicar tried to disabuse him of the notion, 'he continued to harp on this theme, and seemed unable to get rid of it.' (2)

Alerted to Martha's disappearance, Constable Brown made some enquiries around the village, and was soon apprised of the gossip, the consensus being that Buttery had killed Martha and hidden her body in the house. P.C. Brown decided to put the matter in the hands of his immediate superior, Sergeant Gray of Castleton, which meant the inquiry lost another day, and it wasn't until the afternoon of Thursday 28th May that Gray came over to Bradwell to interview Buttery. In the company of P.C. Brown he traced Buttery to his cowhouse and bluntly told him, 'We have heard it rumoured that you have your wife concealed in your house.' (2) James calmly denied it, and assented to the policemen searching his premises, offering to go with them.

After first searching the cowhouse, the officers went to the house and searched the two upstairs and two downstairs rooms thoroughly but found nothing to confirm their suspicions. Buttery 'lent every assistance,' and 'answered everything frankly and openly and did not seem at all flustered,' (2) as Gray was later to testify. Afterwards, whilst Constable Brown examined mine shafts in the area and dragged some ponds, Buttery made a statement, which the sergeant took down:

'James Buttress, farmer and stonemason, of Smalldale, Bradwell. I declare that myself and wife went to bed at nine o'clock at night on April 30th, and on my waking at five o'clock next morning I found my wife had got up. I called out, 'Where are you?' but received no answer. I called out, 'Are you got up?' but still no answer. I then got up, went downstairs and found the door closed and latched, but not locked or bolted as I had locked and bolted it on the previous night before going to bed. The reason why I have not troubled after my wife is because she has gone from home before, but has always returned in a few days. On Saturday, May 2nd, I found she had taken £75 from the recess of a drawer in a writing desk in the house-place, and on Monday, May 4th, I found £100 had been taken from the same drawer, and on Wednesday the 6th, £37.10s. This money I had placed in separate parts of the drawer. I and my wife have had words before, and she has threatened to go to her daughter's.' (2)

Although James may have presented a calm exterior to the police he was feeling the pressure, for others noticed that he grew 'more excited day by day', (4) and took a keen interest in the progress of the search for Martha which was getting under way.

Now that it was official that Martha was missing and that James was the last to see her, and given that he had made threats against her life shortly before she went missing, most people in Smalldale and Bradwell drew the obvious conclusion. Aware of this, James protested his innocence to all he spoke with. On the morning of the day after the search, Friday, 29th May, he told a regular caller, either his brother-in-law or nephew William Bramall (for both bore the same name), that he was anxious for his wife's return and 'that if she only came back he would die contented.' (5) Later in the morning, he called on the Revd. Dudley to ask if he had heard from his daughter, to whom he had written. He told the vicar that he was in distress about the disappearance of his wife, and added that the police had searched his house. He said, 'there's a suspicion against me, and I'm sure there's no need.' (2)

He seems to have been 'sounding out' the vicar, almost as a sample of public opinion, asking, 'what must I do?' The vicar replied, 'I cannot pretend to judge, but if you are innocent, which God knows, you must show the greatest possible activity in the search.' (2) In justification, Buttery said that he had been searching all night for her in the company of his brother-in-law, Robert Middleton, and added that he was going to ask the next day for permission to have water at a nearby mill dam let off to see if Martha's body was there.

By half-past one that afternoon Buttery had turned his steps to the Bowling Green Tavern, but if he was hoping for either help or sympathy from his sister Nancy, he was to be disappointed. Indeed, it could have been his sister's plain-speaking which caused James to make his last, desperate act in the Bradwell Mystery, as it was to be named by the newspapers.

Nancy had been raised very much in the hard-knocks school of life. Before she was eleven years old she was in service at a farm in the Woodlands. At the age of twenty, she gave birth to an illegitimate child, and raised her alone until she married Joseph Bramall four years later. Tragically, Joseph died when only forty-five years old, and subsequently Nancy lost two of her daughters at early ages. No stranger to personal tragedies, she was a battler who believed in facing life head-on, and when James came into her tavern, she faced him directly with the question every villager in Bradwell was asking.

' "Now, Jim, has't thou made away with her?" Nancy asked. "You know it's bound to come out. Now they have begun to search, they will find her, dead or alive. I want you to tell me the truth." ' (2)

'I know nothing about her. I have not seen her since she went out of the house,' her brother replied, and though Nancy 'pressed over and over again,' he doggedly stuck to his story, adding rather selfishly that if Martha was not found soon he would have to get one of his daughters to keep house, as he could not stand it much longer. (2)

Finding no safe haven at the Bowling Green Tavern, Buttery made his way home, a few yards up the lane from the tavern. A neighbour, Sarah Ann Taylor, said she saw him going in at his door, and her testimony that 'he did not speak to her, nor she to him,' (3) probably portrays the general disfavour that James was now regarded with in the village. Sarah Ann did not see or hear anything more of him that day. Alone in his house, with the whole village seemingly turned against him, the searching and the whispering both intensifying, Buttery brooded on it all.

* * * * *

The following morning, Saturday, May 30th, Buttery was not seen at his usual early time, and when, by eight o'clock he was still missing, and it was discovered that his cows had not been milked on Friday evening, William Bramall went to P.C. Brown and reported the matter.

The constable immediately went to the house to investigate. The door was locked, so after some knocking and calling out, he fetched a ladder and forced an entry through an upstairs window.

He found James's lifeless body on the stairs, in a seated position. He had hanged himself by trapping a rope between an upstairs door and the lintel. The body was quite cold and stiff, and James had obviously been dead for some time. P.C. Brown called for help and a man called Luther Hall came up the ladder into the house and helped cut Buttress down.

The constable searched the body and found Buttery's watch, which had stopped at 11.50. The pockets had not been rifled, and there was no sign of any confusion or struggling in the house, confirming to Brown's mind that it was a case of suicide. A note in Buttery's handwriting, which the constable could prove to be the dead man's since it matched the previous note from him, written in Brown's presence, was found and taken for evidence at the inquest.

News of Buttery's death soon spread around Bradwell, and as one paper reported, 'The excitement during the day was intense, crowds of people visiting the place, and many were the surmises as to what he had done with his wife, the locality being very favourable for hiding anything…' (2)

Rumour was indeed rife, and all discussed and examined James's actions during the last month. He had spent much time digging in his garden, and opinion seemed to be split three ways: Martha was down a leadmine shaft, of which there were literally hundreds dotted all over Bradwell Moor; Martha was buried in the garden; third and

P.C. Brown, Bradwell's 'bobby' for thirty years, at the time of his retirement in 1913

most lurid, that Martha was walled up somewhere in the house, which was why she had been missed in the original police search. *The Derbyshire Courier* reported the ghoulish rumour thus:

'It was also noticed that a fireplace in one of the bedrooms had recently been walled up and limewashed. It may here be stated that Buttress, who was a farmer and stonemason, was provided with tools for the purpose. A horrible smell pervades the house, but the police refuse to allow anything to be touched until after the funeral of Buttress.' (7)

So prevalent and macabre were the rumours, that Revd. Dudley made special reference to the case after his sermon on the Sunday. He urged the congregation to not pass judgement 'at any rate at present.' (3) He referred to the inquest to be held the next day, and asked all to pray for the daughters, who were coming to Bradwell as soon as possible.

The inquest was held on Monday afternoon at the Bowling Green Tavern. After the jury and gentlemen of the press had visited the Buttery house, the deputy coroner for the High Peak, Mr. Meggison, jury, witnesses, a solicitor representing the Buttery daughters, and representatives of the press all crowded into a cramped, low-ceilinged room in the sixteenth century tavern. Until the coming of piped water, Bradwell was always short of water in summer. A laxer attitude than that of our times to domestic and personal hygiene, combined with the midden possessed by all households of the day, and the smells from a slaughterhouse next to the tavern all added to a powerful, general aroma in the room. The scene was well described by the correspondent of the *Derbyshire Times*. He managed to dispel the rumour of a body being concealed in the Buttery House and also to get in a waspish swipe at Nancy's tavern in just one line, writing that 'the atmosphere was sweet compared with that in the room where the coroner's inquest was held.' (8)

The first witness called was an older brother of James Buttery. He was William Buttery, licensee of the Cobden View Hotel in Sheffield. He testified that the body he had seen was that of his brother, and that he had last seen James alive on the 14th of May, spending three or four hours with him. James had been in low spirits and told William that Martha had gone away, taking some money with her, but did not say how much. He said that he thought James's 'mind was unhinged' as he 'talked very flighty at times.' (7) Interestingly, William also cast doubts on James's long-term sanity He said that 'it was his impression that his brother had not been right for years – ever since… a cart ran over his head. He believed the moon had a great effect upon him, for he often raved then (when the moon was full).' (7)

Sergeant Grey was the next to give evidence. He testified to interviewing Buttery and taking his statement, and when asked by Mr. Sowter, the Manchester solicitor representing Buttery's daughters, if James had mentioned Martha's supposed infidelity, he said that the deceased had suggested she 'might have eloped with somebody.' (7)

Constable Brown followed. He spoke of the background to the case, of Martha's black eye, and James's earlier allegations against her. He told of finding James dead, and of searching the body and finding the suicide note, addressed to one of Buttery's daughters. A sensation was caused when the coroner read it out:

'Ther is 42 pound in the red bag and 2 cows and 1 calf, for i have lived as long as i care for i cannot hear of her but ther are a good many things to be said. Your hunkel Jo Wright as been making a wife on your mother for this last year.' (7)

Here the coroner broke off and asked the constable, 'Did he ever mention that to you?'

'Yes sir,' Brown replied, 'Many a time.'

Coroner Meggison resumed reading the suicide note: 'And fil (Phil) Middleton and your Ant Elizabeth as been ceping a house of bad fame, for she has taken £212. 10s.' (7)

At this point Meggison decided to verify that the suicide letter was actually written by Buttery and sent P.C. Brown for the letter James had written some months before. When he had compared the letters he broached the subject of the awful allegation in the letter, asking if Constable Brown had interviewed Martha's brother Joseph Wright about the accusation made, that he had been sexually involved with his own sister. The constable said he had not, and when asked why not, said, 'It was not my place, sir.'

'Why not?' persisted the coroner, and the constable stubbornly replied, 'It was not my place.' (7)

Mr. Meggison may not have been aware of it, but he was stirring up a hornet's nest. The majority of people in the room were Bradwell folk, and for centuries intermarriage and closeness of families had been the norm. Nearly everyone in the small Peak village was related in some way to everyone else, and attachment to family was so deep-rooted that as one visitor observed, 'many have been known to have suffered the severest privations rather than tear themselves from this bleak and cheerless village,' (8) Given this closeness to one's kin, what the madly jealous Buttery had frequently alleged and what the coroner appeared to be giving credence to by investigating further, cut deeply.

Still the coroner pressed on with Buttery's slanderous accusation.

'Do you mean to tell me that you suspected murder, and that adultery was the cause of it, and you did not think it your duty to ask any questions of the man whom Buttery supposed, rightly or wrongly to have to do with it?' he asked. (7)

This was too much for one juror. As the constable replied that the allegation 'was before this,' the juror interjected, 'He was her brother; the whole thing was unworthy of credence.' (7)

'It is very monstrous, no doubt,' Mr. Meggison replied, 'but it is no sign of insanity for a man to accuse his wife of that crime.' (7)

At this, the Butterys' daughters' solicitor, Mr. Sowter, intervened and informed the coroner that James's manner was often erratic when accusing his wife, that there were no grounds for supposing that Mrs. Buttery was unfaithful, and he wished that the jury should see that the deceased had both homicidal and suicidal tendencies.

Again a juror interrupted the proceedings. Angered by what was seen as an attack on Martha's good name, he said, ''There have been aspersions cast upon this woman, while her character was quite the reverse. That ought to be made thoroughly plain.' (7) Who the juror was is not known since we have only the foreman of the jury's name. It is quite likely it was the foreman himself who told Meggison off, however, for he was Job Middleton, and the 'Ant Liz' referred to in the suicide note as 'running a house of bad fame' (i.e. a brothel), was the sister to whom Martha turned when she needed a night's shelter from James's violence, and she had married into the Middleton family. Bradwell was a tight little community, as the coroner was discovering!

Sarah Ann Taylor, a neighbour of the Buttery family, was the next witness. She was the last person to see James alive, and she testified, amongst other things, to hearing quarrelling between James and Martha Buttery shortly before Martha disappeared. She, too, was questioned about Martha's alleged infidelity and said that there were no grounds for James's suspicions.

The Revd. H.T. Dudley was then called upon to give evidence. He stated that he knew Buttery well, that the man had at one time been addicted to drink but had been much more temperate lately. Buttery had told him on his last visit to the vicarage that Martha had taken £212 with her, and 'again and again his wife's unfaithfulness came up… he continued to harp upon this theme, and seemed unable to get rid of it.' (7)

Such an educated and clearly unbiased witness was just what both the solicitor and the angry juror were waiting for. Both asked about Buttery's slanders against Martha, and the vicar gave it as his opinion that 'on this one subject … deceased was thoroughly insane.' (7)

The coroner could not allow this to pass, however, saying that he 'did not think that this charge against his wife could be taken as evidence of his insanity. It was known that Queen Anne Boleyn had been accused and found guilty of incest. It was no proof of insanity.' The Revd. Dudley replied, 'It is most unnatural,' and the coroner agreed, 'That may well be.' (7)

Although Mr. Meggison was only attempting to attempting to resist a verdict of insanity being imposed by interested parties, his seeming sympathy towards Buttery's allegations against Martha and her brother, Joseph Wright, rankled with those who knew them well, and someone in that room appears to have gone home and written a letter to the press to relieve his anger, for two days later in the *Sheffield Daily Telegraph* the following communication appeared:

'Sir, Was the coroner at the Bradwell inquest on Monday justified in attempting to weaken Mr. Dudley's evidence by a reference to the case of Queen Anne Boleyn?… She was tried in secret, and condemned in secret, and the trumped-up nature of this charge was shown by the King marrying Jane Seymour on the third day after her execution – some say the day after. Those who know

Bradwell and Smalldale people want no further evidence of Buttery's insanity upon this point than that furnished by the letter found in his pocket, in which the most utterly groundless charges are laid against highly moral and respectable people. Yours faithfully, N. Z.' (6)

The Revd. Dudley was the last witness at the inquest, but Mr. Sowter, the solicitor for the Buttery daughters, felt that the question of Buttery's sanity had still not been fully examined. He desired, he said, to make it perfectly clear that Buttery had had homicidal tendencies. The letter, which was 'the last thing the deceased did,' (7) was proof. Sowter stated that he could produce evidence to show that the man had previously attempted suicide, for which there was also medical proof. At this the jury asked if they could retire to consider 'whether they would hear further evidence as to the state of the deceased's mind at the time of committing the act.' (7) The coroner allowed this, but summed up before the jury left the room.

They were out for a long time, and when they did return the foreman, Job Middleton, handed the coroner a piece of paper, returning their unanimous verdict that 'Matthew James Buttery has hanged himself whilst in an insane state of mind.' (7)

But where was Martha? That was the question on everyone's mind, and on this the jury had something to say also, recommending, again to a man, that 'a more strenuous effort should be made to find the missing woman,' (7) and with this at least the coroner agreed. Mr. Sowter, speaking for the relatives, said that every effort would now be made to unravel the mystery. Handbills would be issued, and a reward offered, and he called on the people of Bradwell to assist the police, who would have much to do. The coroner gave an order for the internment of Buttery's body, and the inquest was over. The other, unofficial inquest into Martha's fate was to continue for much longer.

* * * * *

James Buttery's funeral took place on the following day, Tuesday, June 2nd. 1885. The coffin was first carried to the Bowling Green Tavern, a place which must have contributed much to the misery of both James and Martha. Here the mourners were assembled, a small group of close family, for James had left few friends, it seems. There was a custom in Bradwell at the time for the singers and musicians of the village to attend a funeral procession and chant a solemn dirge on the way to the church, with the rest of the company joining in the responses (coincidentally this was last performed in 1900, when the foreman of the jury at James's inquest, Job Middleton, was buried), but James doesn't seem to have been accorded this rite, further evidence of how much of an outcast he remained, even in death. Yet the case was the sensation of the area, and nearly everyone in the village turned out for the funeral. As the coffin was carried to St. Barnabas's Church, groups of villagers assembled to see it pass, whilst in the vicinity of the churchyard a large crowd had gathered. Because Buttery had committed the mortal sin of suicide, his remains were not allowed inside the church, the service being held at the graveside, and the gentlemen of the press were there to record it:

'It was simple and plain… reverently read by the Rev. H.T. Dudley… The brightness of the summer afternoon failed to relieve the sadness of the spectacle. The anguish of the daughters, as they leaned upon each other, sobbing out their grief, was painful to witness.' (H)

The grave was dug to the depth of seven feet because it was to be a joint grave; it was expected by most of Bradwell that Martha's remains, once found, would shortly follow those of her husband to their last and, finally, peaceful resting place. But first, Martha had to be found.

Police Superintendent Hallam of Chapel-en-le-Frith now took personal charge of the inquiry into Martha's disappearance, and with the assistance of Sergeant Gray, Constable Brown, and a new man drafted into the search, a P.C. Seeley of Bamford, he set out on a trail that was a month cold.

Firstly they searched the house the couple had lived in together. Despite the Buttery daughters' assurances that a fireplace in one of the bedrooms had been bricked up for years, the police broke into it and inserted a long pole, without finding anything. A writing desk was more productive, yielding many papers, including rough drafts of letters which Buttery had sent to his daughters. In these he begged them to tell him where their mother was if they knew, swearing that he could not live without her. In other documents there was 'ample evidence that he intended to commit suicide,' (H) and repeated allegations against Martha and her brother. Also found were documents in which he recorded his daily transactions. Although rough and ready, they purported to show that a few days before Martha's disappearance he had given her a sum of about £210 to take care of. With such a fortune, some newspapers reasoned, Martha could be lying low in one of the Midland cities or towns, or some remote spot where she was not known.

If Martha *had* fled her husband's rages she had travelled light, for a thorough search of the house revealed that 'all her clothes and linen were carefully laid by in boxes, excepting a common print dress and a bonnet of the same material which Mrs. Buttery was in the habit of wearing day by day.' (12) No one at this stage seems to have thought Martha was alive, however. Indeed, most expected the search to be a short one, culminating in the discovery of Martha's remains. Willing volunteers, enthusiastic in the first flush of the search, helped the police in their examination of the area surrounding the Buttery house. Iron rods were used to probe two plots of land where Buttery had turned up rows to sow turnips, but nothing came to light. Attention was then paid to finding a supposed well in the Butterys' garden but probes of the ground did not locate the presence of any well.

Meanwhile, Superintendent Hallam had decided to interview Martha's brother, Joseph Wright, but he at first refused to attend an interview and had to be reminded that one did not say no to the police! He eventually presented himself and was questioned by Hallam and Mr. Sowter. Whether his feelings were soothed, or he was threatened with the full severity of the law if he did not co-operate is not known, but there was a marked change of attitude on his part, and he 'stated his willingness to furnish any information in his power.' (8) Nothing of any importance was learned, though, save that there had been bad blood between him and his brother-in-law for some time, probably as a result of Buttery's allegations.

At ten o'clock that evening the searchers turned their attention to the isolated shippon in the field, towards which Martha had been heading with James when last seen. Here the search party of police and leadminers, under the direction of the Superintendent, set to work. They shovelled out about three tons of manure and turned it over, examining it closely. Nothing was found in it, but then the first real clue came to light when the shippon had been cleared and some wooden 'boskins' or partitions were taken away. Under a pile of hay seeds the searchers found a pair of Martha's boots. These were good, almost new, boots, not cast-offs, and were identified as a pair which she had worn daily in her work. This find, of course, suggested that Martha may well have been murdered there, in the shippon. Also found nearby was 'a large maul or hammer, such as stone-getters use… The hammer is very rusty, but on the head are some dark red stains, which are thought to be too dark for rust. However, the building has been most carefully overhauled, and no distinct indication of any foul play having taken place in it has been discovered.' (9)

This discovery of the boots put new heart into the searchers, and they took up the wooden floor of the building and dug down to a depth of two feet or so, but it was obvious that nothing – or no one – had been hidden there. Much play was made by some newspapers of a 'suspicious-looking rope' which was found in the shippon. This was made into a double noose and given that Buttery had once made an attempt to take Martha's life by hanging her, and had eventually hanged himself, it did at first seem significant. The rope ceased to have been regarded as of any significance, however, when it was pointed out that it had most probably been used for tying up a calf the Buttery's owned. However, just because the rope was there for one purpose doesn't mean it wasn't utilized for another, deadlier purpose, just as the hammer could have been used for more than breaking stone. However, forensics was in it its infancy in those days, so there was no testing that could be done, and the items have to be merely pointed out as having been there.

The searchers worked on as the light failed, and after thoroughly scouring the shippon they wanted, although it was after ten-thirty, to examine a well on the Buttery property. As they had been working by lantern-light for some time, Hallam ruled it out, and dismissed the party until the next day. Before leaving for home at Chapel-en-le-Frith, he and Mr. Sowter engaged a group of seven leadminers to begin a search of the old mine shafts and workings the following day. The Superintendent also visited the local blacksmith and commissioned the making of a grisly item for use by the miners. It was to be an iron rod, several yards in length, with long, sharp spikes at one end, so that when the search party of miners descended a flooded shaft they could probe the water at the bottom for a possible body below the surface.

Wednesday, June 3rd dawned hot and clear, and the mood in the search party was one of optimism. They expected to find Martha's body close to home, and since a blank had been drawn at the Buttery house and the shippon' they reasoned that the most likely place of concealment left was one of the many mineshafts on the outskirts of the village. To this end, the party of miners was directed to explore Nunley Rake, a long strip of old abandoned mineshafts in Smalldale, which followed the course of a great vein of lead, many of the shafts having caved in or being in dangerous condition.

The system for searching was very primitive. One miner sat on a piece of wood attached to a length of rope and was lowered down by the others by means of a windlass, his search illuminated only by lantern light. This crude method meant that only the safer mines could be examined, and many of the very old shafts, whose lining walls were crumbling or even partially blocked received only a cursory examination.

Quite soon one of the miners reported finding a full sack down one of the shafts, and this caused some excitement among the police and other helpers on the surface. Their high hopes were soon dashed, though, when the 'sack' turned out to be a heap of rotten timbers. After investigating about twenty likely mines with no success, the men were called off.

Wells in the area were dragged with grappling hooks, and gardens dug over, including a garden Buttery had cultivated across from his home which ran alongside Joseph Wright's house. Almost two hours were spent in fruitless digging and the mood of optimism was beginning to evaporate as the search spread wider.

At half-past four that afternoon Superintendent Hallam arrived in the village in his four-wheeled dog cart, with an unusual helper, a cross-breed Mastiff-St Bernard dog called Bruce, which is described as having a strong touch of 'blood' in it. It was hoped to 'discover the missing woman in the event of her having become exhausted and perished in her flight from her husband.' (12) It was still known for travellers in the area to become lost or overcome and die on the high moors around Bradwell, though usually only in winter. Martha had been gone for a month, however, and Bruce failed to detect any useful scent around the Buttery house which would give him a trail to follow.

Disappointed once more, Hallam turned his attention to the house again, and examined the walls and floors minutely for any clues. On the walls of the living room were several framed prints of the type beloved by the Victorian. One, of a child guarded by a dog, was titled 'Fidelity', another of a lamb was titled 'Innocence', both bitterly ironic when one considers the foul suspicions Buttery had allowed to poison his mind against Martha. 'Happy Christmas' adorned another wall, while over the mantelpiece of the bedroom which Buttery claimed Martha so left so stealthily while he slept, never to be seen again, was 'The Flight into Egypt', yet another irony. Had Martha truly fled, the police were frequently to ask each other during the investigation? Was Buttery innocent? This last was a belief one of them was to cling to in the face of disbelief and resistance from others who knew the missing woman and her habits much better than any member of the investigating team.

In the living room, the police thought that the mortar between the flagstones of the hearth looked fresh. Bearing in mind that Buttery was a stonemason and skilled stonewaller, and considered 'very natty at his job' (2), the thought arose that perhaps Martha had been concealed there. Seats were lifted, the flagstones raised, and the earth beneath them was dug up, to no avail.

The following morning, Thursday, June 4th, brought another hot summer's day, but if the search party was hoping to slacken the pace a little in the heat, they were to be disappointed, for Captain Parry, the Chief Constable of Derbyshire, descended on the village. Quite why he did so is not known now. Perhaps the reported failure of the police appointed to investigate Martha's disappearance to come up with any concrete evidence had nettled him, perhaps the delay in investigating the murder occasioned criticism of the local force at a higher level than the foreman's jury. At any event, Captain Parry took charge of the investigation for the duration of his visit.

At times it must have seemed to the searchers that James Buttery had set them some sort of giant puzzle as they searched the valley sides and up onto the moors for the body of Martha. Some may have even begun to try and put themselves into the crazed man's mind, for it was recalled that James had told another villager that Martha 'was no more than a mile away from here,' (3) that he had told someone else that he had dreamed of Martha and the shaft of the old Cronstadt Mine up on Gawtrey Hill. It seemed as if he had been telling people to look for her there.

The agent for the Cronstadt Mine was questioned and said that he 'knew for certain that someone had partially removed the stones, there being an aperture large enough to admit a human body.' (9) A Mr. George Bamford lent a powerful crab, a kind of winch, and a very experienced leadminer, an old man named Robert Pearson bravely made a very tricky descent of 240 feet (73metres) down the shaft, which was in bad repair, having been closed for around fifty years or more. He spent some time in the workings, reporting them perfectly dry, but found nothing. Had Buttery deliberately left the searchers a red herring to follow? Was he mocking them from the grave? It must have felt like it to the search party as they sweltered on the bare flanks of Bradwell Moor. In the afternoon another mine, called Windy Mine was examined with no success, and by now the stamina and morale of the searching miners was beginning to flag:

'They were much exhausted, as they had been exerting themselves under a burning sun for two-and-a-half days. As long as there were any likely places unexplored they laboured most commendably, buoyed up with the hope that success might shortly crown their effort.' (11)

Captain Parry pronounced himself pleased with everything done so far, decided to release the miners from their duties, and they were paid off by Mr. Sowter, 'at least for a day or two'. (11)

There seems to have been a financial consideration at work here, too, as two days later Mr. Sowter expressed a hope that local miners would volunteer to search some of the mines without payment, but they in turn said that it would be 'certain death to venture down some of the tremendous gulfs, and also that whilst

Mrs. Buttery's relatives hold aloof and decline to assist in the search, it cannot be expected of others.' (13) Quite who the miners meant is not specified, but Martha's brother Joseph does not appear in any report as being involved in a search party, and even had to be put under duress before assenting to being interviewed by the police. Maybe the unnamed relatives and the miners were being realistic about the chances of thoroughly exploring underground, however, for one newspaper acknowledged that 'An exhaustive search of every boring (mineshaft), many of them being forgotten and unknown, would have been an endless and probably an impossible task.' (13)

However, the Buttery daughters had a problem. Until Martha was proven to be dead they could not legally inherit what property was left. None of them was wealthy, and the costs of the solicitor and the search party would not have been cheap. Again, Joseph Wright could have helped financially if he had wished. When he died eight years later, and his household effects were up for auction, a secret drawer in an old box yielded up a hoard of gold, a bank note, and a large quantity of silver coins. More money was also found hidden all over his house. One would have thought that he could have spared a little of his fortune to have helped his nieces and tried to find the remains of his sister, but both he and Martha were known to be tight-fisted with money, and he does not seem to have done so.

It was at this stage of the enquiry that for some reason Superintendent Hallam appears to have reached the conclusion that Martha had not been murdered, but left the house of her own accord, and he freely gave this as his opinion to the newspapers of the day. They generally reported that it was not an opinion shared by the villages, however, 'who firmly affirm that a murder has been committed.' Quite what evidence Hallam had for his opinion is never given; possibly it was 'negative proof', born out of frustration with the search and lack of results. If Martha could not be found she must have left the valley and be in hiding somewhere, would seem to have been his line of reasoning.

It has to be admitted that there were precedents for people in the area disappearing when the occasion suited. The *Sheffield Daily Telegraph* quoted two instances of people from the area disappearing, only to show up alive later, in support of their statement that while the Bradwell folk believed Martha dead, others in the surrounding area were expecting her to be found alive and hiding out from her husband's wrath:

Whether the missing Martha has wandered away, and, in her inability to read or write, remains blissfully ignorant of how largely she figures in Derbyshire story, or has really been murdered and is hidden down a disused shaft, remains as great a mystery as on the morning Buttery was found self-strangled at the back of his own door. Bradwell and Smalldale generally believe the worst, but away from that quarter, at Hope and Brough, and Bamford and Hathersage, people think differently. They recall the Hope saddler, who disappeared as mysteriously and suddenly, was not seen for months, and then turned up as quietly and unconcernedly as if he had been teaching Sunday School in some more remote part of the Peak. And it afterwards turned out that… he had not been half-a-dozen miles from home all the time. He had lived in the woods and caves, returning in the dead of night to his own house for food, the strange removal of which never seemed to excite any suspicion. The man is living yet. And then they tell of another "Derbyshire Mystery," which is stranger still. A tenant farmer went to pay his rent. He was seen to go up Bradwell Dale, and then – all trace was lost. The popular belief was that he had been waylaid and murdered for the money he had with him; the dams were dragged, the mines explored, the mountains and valleys searched. Nothing came of it. Five years later a Bradwell lad found his way to Malta, and there, drilling as a soldier, was the missing man. The clue to this mystery was clear enough. He had spent the money without paying the rent, and seeing no easy way out of the difficulty he took the shilling and became a "bowd sowjer boy." So you see that, even in Derbyshire Mysteries there is nothing new under the sun.' (14)

Strange tales, but it has to be said that Bradwell and Smalldale folk knew their own, and their opinion that Martha was dead was based on more than a couple of previous disappearances of other people. Martha was old and infirm, and her husband had laid hands on her before, and made threats to kill her. It was the most obvious explanation.

More gardens were dug over on the Friday, and on Saturday two dams at Somerset's cotton spinning mill between Bradwell and the nearby hamlet of Brough were drained and examined. Buttery had been observed on several nights in succession heading towards the dams, carrying a bag and contents, a relative claimed, so hopes were raised once more. Some bones found in the bottom of one dam caused a flurry of excitement but were soon found to be those of a dog. A few days later a reservoir below the dam was also drained in case the body had washed down from the dams, but again nothing was found.

Mr. Sowter was present at the dams on Saturday and told a reporter that he was in communication with a number of friends and was trying to obtain a pure bloodhound. The newspaper, probably recalling the dog Bruce's lack of success, seemed to be unimpressed, adding, 'beyond this, he has done nothing.' (15)

The village did not intend to give up on rumour and gossip, though, even if it had given up searching. Further excitement was caused when someone claimed that the grave of George Bradwell had been tampered with. Turfs had been lifted, it was asserted. This was the grave of the old man whose funeral had touched off the Butterys' last argument, and some thought that maybe James had carried Martha's body though the village in the middle of the night to the Wesleyan cemetery and buried her there with George. It was a mark of how desperate the search was becoming. Iron rods were fetched, and the grave prodded with them, but there proved to be only one occupant in the grave.

At five o'clock that afternoon the Superintendent again visited the village and made enquiries around the area concerning the £212 Martha was supposed to have taken with her when she left. He announced that he had communicated with several police superintendents 'as to the procuring of a bloodhound', to help in the search, and was keeping the Buttery house locked up so that 'a scent, if any, may not be interfered with.' (15) Clearly, he was grasping at straws. Later, he went to see a man who sparked off yet another rumour about the mystery, a farmer called Henry Eyre.

The tale being repeated around Bradwell was that Eyre was walking back to his home at the splendidly named Burster Bottom between Tideswell and Bradwell on the night that Martha disappeared. It was after midnight when he chanced upon James Buttery, close to a limekiln in Bradwell Dale, a narrow gorge through which the main road to the village winds. Buttery was carrying a large sack bag which was so heavy he had to pause to rest, and the sack was 'reared against a wall'. Eyre said he had spoken to James, whom he knew well, but to his surprise Buttery ignored him. Given that Martha was a small, slight woman, and James a large, strong man, one can guess what the villagers thought James had in the bag.

The story was wrong, however, in two vital aspects. The first was that the bag was only a small one, so small that Buttery carried it over his arm. The second, that the night on which Eyre met Buttery was the night before Martha had disappeared. Eyre was adamant on this point, as he had gone over to Woodlands to discuss a pending lawsuit and had recorded the appointment in his diary.

Despite the errors, this switched the investigation to the other end of the village. The limekiln was examined, and Luther Morton, the proprietor, said that tons of lime had been removed in the last month, but 'nothing extraordinary had been observable'. (13) Nearby there were several abandoned mine shafts in Bradwell Dale, but the covering on none of them showed any signs of being disturbed. Later in the week the extensive horizontal flues of the smelting works, which ran into the sides of the dale, some of them several hundred yards long, were examined, dogs being taken to the openings to 'sniff them', but again a blank was drawn.

After the interview with Eyre, Superintendent Hallam had a long interview with Joseph Wright once more. He was accompanied to Wright's house, across the lane from the Buttery's cottage, at a late hour, by Sergeant Gray and Mr. Sowter. The house was thoroughly searched, 'a proceeding which surprised Wright exceedingly.' (16) He protested that he did not know what had happened to his sister, and when he was asked if, had Martha gone away, she would have taken her money with her, he remarked that, 'she must have done, as when the money was divided she had the largest share.' (16) Presumably he was talking about the division of property and assets made when their mother had died twenty-five years ago, with, possibly, Martha taking the money and Joseph the farm.

Hallam was floundering. He had no leads, no further ideas, and pinned his hopes on Martha having left the village alive, as James had said. To this end, Hallam had advertised the disappearance of Martha quite widely. He had caused handbills to be circulated 'through the country', sending copies to police stations and other centres, as well as to workhouse masters; a notice appeared in the *Police Gazette* a weekly newspaper produced by the Home Office and the Metropolitan Police, and in many of the local and county newspapers, giving a thorough description of Martha:

'ADVERTISEMENT: FIVE HUNDRED POUNDS REWARD! MISSING from her home at Bradwell, Derbyshire, since the 1st May, a married woman named Martha Buttress, aged 60, height, about 5ft 5in.; brown hair, going gray, blue eyes, thin features, and slender build; hair looped down under one ear in a coil; mouth slightly drawn on one side by stroke; ears pierced, but no earrings; mole on shoulder; wore, when last seen, an old black dress and white and red plaided handkerchief; also may have on a soft linen bonnet.

'Any person giving such information as will lead to the finding of the above-named person will receive the Reward.

'Apply to CHARLES PEARSON SOWTER, solicitor, Bradwell; or at Holly Mount, Flexton Road, Flexton, Manchester; or to the Superintendent of Police, Chapel-en-le-Frith.'

A reduced search continued into the second week of June. Mr. Sowter, Sergeant Gray and the constables, Brown and Seeley were out every day, and 'indefatigable in their efforts to find her', (13) but with no real direction, the search was dying on its feet. Indeed, it was asked in some quarters whether the ratepayers of the county should be put to any further expense in the endeavour to find Martha Buttery. One newsaper compared the disappearance to other mysteries one could never find the answer to: 'The missing woman at Bradwell remains almost as perplexing a puzzle as the Sphinx… or that conundrum, which was so good that the man who made it, after endeavouring for two and a half years to find out what it meant, gave it up, and cut his throat in utter despair.' (19) Another newspaper put the case with brutal insensitivity, saying that if she were alive Martha would turn up eventually, if she was dead, would be buried when found, and if he did do away with his own wife, James Buttery was, 'by his own hand, beyond the hangman's noose.' (17)

*　*　*　*　*

Then, on Thursday, June 11th, came a new development which must have seemed to everyone involved to be the break they been waiting for: an eye-witness who claimed to have seen a woman answering Martha's description, outside of the Hope Valley, and on the morning Buttery claimed his wife had disappeared.

A woman named Allford, who had read the 'missing from home' advertisement so widely circulated, claimed that on the morning of May 1st, just before six in the morning, she looked out of her bedroom window which overlooked the road that ran between Chapel-en-le-Frith and New Mills and saw an elderly woman matching Martha's description pass by, heading towards Manchester. She wore a black dress with two tucks near the bottom, and a soft bonnet similar to the one Mrs. Buttery was known to wear. She carried a stick to help her walk and seemed footsore. Mrs. Allford's home at Bugsworth (now known as Buxworth) was a walk from Bradwell of around ten miles. Given that Buttery claimed to have woken on that morning at five o'clock and found his wife gone, then Martha may have left at first light of early morning and could have been passing Mrs. Allford's house at just that time. It all fitted and was what the hard-pressed police on the case needed. Hallam jumped at it and began to cast his net further afield.

Two bodies also turned up that week, one of an elderly woman who had died of starvation in an empty house in Higher Buxton Streeet, Manchester. The description matched that of Martha, and Mr. Sowter accompanied one of the Buttery daughters when she went to view the body but did not identify it as being that of her mother. Even Scotland was not too far away for Hallam, for he made enquiries of the police in Forfarshire, where a body was found in King William Docks harbour at Dundee, but again it was not the elusive Martha.

Still Superintendent Hallam stuck to his belief that Martha had left the valley and was either in hiding, or so far away by then, and being unable to read, was not aware that her danger was past with the death of her husband, and that she was being searched for. He made further enquiries and told the press that he was satisfied that the woman seen by Mrs. Allford was Martha Buttery. He claimed to have traced the woman sighted to Furness Dale, two miles further on from Buxworth. It was situated on the direct railway line to Manchester, and 'Here all trace was lost, a matter easily accounted for by the fact that there are several trains running on the Buxton branch of the London and North-Western line in the direction of Stockport and Manchester.' (18)

Another week passed with no more sightings or leads of any kind, and on June 20th the *High Peak News* reported that the local search 'was altogether given up'. (20) As July came in, the daughters had left the village and the windows of the Buttery cottage were boarded up, leaving it to be visited only by 'numbers of excursionists', and 'eager inquirers who assert their reasons for "imagining" or "fancying" Mrs. Buttery is either "buried here", "built up there", "burnt to ashes" somewhere else, or making some other superstitious remark.' (21) Superintendent Hallam still visited the village for a while, but eventually even he had to admit defeat, though continuing to assert that Martha had not been killed by James and her body disposed of locally.

And there the matter rested until February of the following year, 1885, when a man in a Buxton public house told a very strange tale indeed. The man's name was James Needham, an elderly travelling hawker. On the night of Thursday, February 18th, he was staying in a cheap lodging house in Water Lane, Sheffield, and there claimed he encountered Martha Buttery, whom he said he immediately recognised, as he had at one time lived in Bradwell. She was staying there with two travelling hawkers, 'Scotchmen', and when Needham, also known as Twig, Jimmy Twig, or Jimmy Wagg, challenged the woman, she admitted to him that she was indeed Martha, and gave him a shilling to keep quiet, telling him that she only intended staying in Sheffield until the end of the week. It took Needham a week to walk to Buxton, and when he told his tale in the bar of the Rising Sun, in Higher Buxton, the locals quite rightly insisted that he inform the police. The police kept him overnight, and Superintendent Hallam interviewed him the following morning. Needham stuck to his story, and gave a very accurate description of the woman he spoke to, including the fact that her mouth was held a little to one side, and there was a perceptible 'twitch' when she spoke, the result of a stroke, no doubt, and we know that Martha had suffered a slight stroke.

Police Constable Brown escorted Needham to Sheffield that day, and in the company of a Sheffield detective they visited Reynold's Lodging House, Water Lane. The lodging house keeper confirmed Needham's description of the woman, and said that while she and the two hawkers were there they had kept very much to themselves, 'their intention undoubtedly being not to attract attention.' (22) They did not say where they were headed, but from Needham's description of the two men, it was known by the police that 'they have been in the habit of hawking at Bradwell', (22) which would explain how Martha could have fallen in with them, if indeed the mystery women was indeed Martha.

The next Wednesday Superintendent Hallam visited the Ship Yard, Water Lane and spoke with the deputy landlady, who had waited upon the two travellers and their female companion. She told them that the woman was of a superior class to the kind of person who usually lodged there, that she seemed more intimate with the younger of the two hawkers, and upon leaving she paid the bill for all three. Although the hawker Needham had not been able to remember what the old woman had been wearing, the deputy landlady told Hallam that it was a black dress, which was indeed what Martha had on when she disappeared. She also said that the woman had a 'drawn mouth' as if she had suffered a stroke, which was similar to the description of Martha. The Superintendent left Sheffield with 'stronger convictions than before that the woman seen… was none other than Mrs. Buttery.' (23)

If Superintendent Hallam thought Martha Buttery was the woman in the lodging house with the Scottish pedlars, the folks who had known her best didn't think so. One paper reported: 'The Bradwell people consider that, even if it were possible for the woman to be alive (which is most unlikely), she would never venture so near home as Sheffield, where scores of persons from Bradwell live.' (24) Another newspaper put local opinion even more bluntly: 'The general belief at Bradwell is that Mrs. Buttery was murdered and put in the lime kiln in the night time by her husband, and burnt to ashes.' (25) This was a prevalent opinion in Bradwell for some years, as the same 1889 newspaper reported that 'Some neighbours went so far as to say that one night they detected a strange smell from the kiln.' (25)

Following on from this development a Miss Hardy, a young woman living at Castleton, came forward, saying that a fortnight after Martha Buttery's disappearance, she had seen her on several occasions in the same neighbourhood of Sheffield as that of the lodging house.

Superintendent Hallam was convinced that he had located Martha. He circulated police in the area, giving them news of the sighting and a description of the three travellers. It seemed that his earlier claims that Martha was alive would be vindicated, but from that time on, nothing more was heard of the little group of hawkers.

Slowly the rumour and speculation surrounding the Bradwell Mystery began to fade, although it was revived briefly three years later in 1889, when a body was found in a stream at Brough. Interest swiftly died when it proved to be the remains of a tramp who had been in the neighbourhood some days before, however, and soon the people of Bradwell put from their minds the strange case of the woman who had disappeared, as if into thin air. Two years after James killed himself, his house and property were auctioned off at the Castle Hotel in Castleton. The house and outbuildings were sold for £37 and 10 shillings to Mr. Joseph Wright, the man James hated so much, Martha's brother.

*   *   *   *   *

So, did James kill Martha, or did she truly escape the vile insults and violent attacks, to make a new life for herself elsewhere? Let us examine what evidence there is.

First, James Buttery's behaviour before Martha's disappearance: he had threatened her life shortly before she disappeared, and she had told a neighbour that she feared for her very life.

Secondly, James behaviour after she disappeared. Martha had left James before, and he had always sought her out and persuaded her to come home. On this occasion, however, until other people began searching and rumours began to fly, he did nothing, almost as if he had known she was not going to return this time. And why could he not enjoy a full night's sleep, rising early each morning, long before his neighbours? Why did he avoid the upstairs bedroom, choosing instead to pass each night on the sofa downstairs? What of his claim that Martha was no more than a mile away? All these actions point to a deed having been committed which weighed heavily on his mind, to a conscience which would not let him rest.

Thirdly, Martha herself: if she did escape James' clutches, why did she not take any clothes other than those on her back with her? The fact that she was never found would indicate that if she did go of her own accord she had planned her flight well. If so, why flee empty-handed, leaving all her clothes packed away at home? And what, if she did walk out on James, did she wear on her feet? Her boots were found hidden in the shippon, and Martha was notoriously mean with her money. Is it likely that she would have discarded an almost new pair of boots in the shippon, and why were they hidden under a pile of hayseeds? Remember that James had once sent Martha to the shippon where he told her later that he had intended to kill her, and the last sighting of Martha was of her, in the company of James, heading toward the same building.

Fourthly, the money. Much was made of it. Indeed, it is crucial, and the various accounts that James gave of it suggest that he was lying about Martha making off with a small fortune in her possession. The first time that the money is mentioned is when his brother William visited him. James told him that Martha had left him a fortnight previously, that she had taken 'some money', but he did not mention the amount taken. Yet the exact amount is something which he invariably stresses later, and according to his statement to the police, by the time of William's visit he knew exactly how much it was to the last penny.

At first, James claimed that the money was in his keeping, and that he did not realise the full extent of his loss, as he had placed it in three different drawers in his desk. Why would he have kept it separate, and why when he missed the first amount of money, on the 2nd May, did he wait two days before checking the second drawer which had contained money? Even more difficult to believe is his claim that having found the money missing from the second drawer, he waited another two days before discovering that the third and final sum was missing from another drawer in the same desk. It is beyond belief that he would have treated what was a small fortune in those days so off-handedly.

Later, James again changed his story about the missing money, saying in a written statement found after his death that he had given it to Martha to keep. He seems to have been perfecting a story to add strength to the claim that Martha had run away with enough money to start a new life somewhere, changing the story until it sounds credible, but in the process forgetting what the previous version was. As the saying goes, one needs a good memory to be a good liar.

A final point on the money is that James did not seem to care in the month that his wife was missing, that she had taken so much money with her. Rather than bewailing his loss and searching frantically for it, and his wife, James did very little. We know that he was mean with his money. Was such a cavalier attitude to being suddenly almost destitute in keeping with his character?

The most obvious conclusion is that there wasn't any money missing, that it was merely an invention on James's part, to make Martha's disappearance slightly credible, and to support this we have some very powerful evidence indeed – Martha's own testimony.

Some years earlier, Buttery had started up a carting business which failed, losing in the process most of the money which Martha had inherited from her mother. Not long before she went missing, Martha had told a neighbour that when the business had been wound up they had owed £70 on a corn bill, but had now cleared that debt, 'she affirmed, with a kind of pride that they did not owe sixpence in Bradwell or Smalldale.' (26) A few days later she told a neighbour that only £40 was remaining of the fortune she had brought to the marriage. It was also known that she and James had sold a calf that spring, and since James left £42 in the red box and almost twelve shillings in his pockets at the time of his death, Martha's accounting rings a lot truer than James's.

What then of the sightings of Martha made by Mrs. Allford, the hawker, Needham, and Miss Hardy?

Mrs. Allford's sighting of a woman she thought to be Martha was made from an upstairs window of her house, not close to. Further, we are not told how Mrs. Allford could be so certain, six weeks after Martha's disappearance, that May 1st was the day on which she sighted someone answering Martha's description passing her house, nor even what it was about Martha's appearance which stuck in her mind. It was not unusual for country folk to be astir so early, and our ancestors daily walked distances that would make us gasp, literally, so that it could have been any country woman on her way to the railway station in the long, black dress that was common wear in those days. And as people at the time pointed out, if Martha did walk out of the valley, why did no one else see her until she was ten miles away? It was a spring morning; farmers and their labourers would have been out and about, and Martha was well enough known in the area. It seems impossible for her to have passed unnoticed out of the Hope Valley.

As to Needham the hawker, there is something which does not quite ring true when one looks at his account. First, there is the delay of four days in telling his story. If he truly believed that he had seen Martha, why did he not tell the police in Sheffield, or as soon as he reached Buxton? He was eager enough to try and claim the reward later. As to the fact that he claimed to know Martha from the days when he lived in Bradwell, he had left that place fifty years before, when Martha would have been ten years old! What seems more likely is that he had seen a woman who looked somewhat like Martha's description in the circulated 'woman missing' advertisements and spun a bar room tale some days later at Buxton, possibly after a few drinks – maybe even to try and gain some more – and once he had committed himself to the lie, had to stick to it. Perhaps he even believed the woman he saw at the lodging house in Sheffield was Martha, and embellished the tale by saying that she had admitted it to him, had temporarily bought his silence with a shilling.

Miss Hardy's sightings of Martha in Sheffield a fortnight after she had disappeared are very strange, her silence over the months during the search hard to explain. When she first saw Martha, Miss Hardy may not have known that Martha was missing from home, but after the rumours started to circulate, why did she not tell someone that she had seen Martha? Surely it would have only been natural to have confided in somebody? Certainly, after James killed himself and the police began to investigate, it was Miss Hardy's duty to inform them of what she knew. What seems most likely is that she never saw Martha at all, but was merely seeking attention, to 'get her name in the papers'.

There is also the 'negative evidence'. Martha was not definitely seen or heard of since the night of April 30th, yet she was a true native of Bradwell. She had never been away from her village and was, as everyone who knew her stressed, exceptionally fond of her daughters. If she had really been alive, would she not have attempted to get in touch with them, to let them know she was well and ease their worries? It would have been a terribly cruel thing to do, to leave with never another word, and let those she loved so dearly wonder for the rest of their lives what had happened to her. Wouldn't she, at least once in her wanderings with her 'Scotch pedlars', have revisited her beloved village? She had committed no crime, after all.

It seems when one looks back at all the available reports that the only people who believed that Martha escaped and made a new life elsewhere were the police, and for 'police' read Superintendent Hallam, who must have been under a lot of pressure to produce something at the end of the investigation to justify the expense incurred and the man-hours involved in the search. The majority of people in Bradwell and Smalldale who knew Martha and James intimately after living cheek by jowl with the pair for so many years believed that 'The strongest probability is that she is dead and buried somewhere in the land and the grass is growing over her'. (26) Proof that even James's immediate family believed James to be a murderer is shown by their never having a memorial of any description placed over his grave. To this day, he lies in an unmarked grave.

One final, eerie fact which points to Martha having met a violent end surfaced during research for this final chapter: at the inquest, you may recall, William Buttery gave evidence that since sustaining injuries in a carting accident some years previously, his brother James had 'not been right', and that 'the moon had a great effect

Buttery's House more recently

upon him, for he often raved then.' (7)

Almanacs for the year of 1885 show that there was a full moon on April 28th, two nights before Martha disappeared, and again on the night of May 27th, two nights before James Buttery killed himself and took the answer to the Bradwell Mystery to his unmarked grave in St Barnabas's churchyard.

REFERENCES

1. *Bradwell: Ancient and Modern* by Seth Evans,
      Broad Oaks Press, 1912. Reprinted by Country Books 2014.
2. *The Sheffield Daily Telegraph*, Tuesday 2nd June 1885.
3. *The Sheffield and Rotherham Independent*, Wednesday 3rd June 1885.
4. *The Sheffield and Rotherham Independent*, Monday 1st June. 1885
5. *The Derby Daily Telegraph*, Friday 5th June.
6. *The Sheffield Daily Telegraph* Wednesday 3rd June 1885.
7. *The Sheffield Daily Telegraph* Tuesday 2nd June 1885.
8. *The Derbyshire Times and Chesterfield Herald*,
      Wednesday 3rd June 1885.
9. *The Sheffield and Rotherham Independent,* Friday 5th June 1885.
10. *The Sheffield and Rotherham Independent*, Saturday 6th June 1885.
11. *The Nottingham Evening Post,* Saturday 6th June 1885.
12. *The Sheffield and Rotherham Independent*, Thursday 4th June 1885.
13. *The Sheffield and Rotherham Independent*, Monday 8th June 1885.
14. *The Sheffield Daily Telegraph*, Thursday 18th June 1885.
15. *The Nottingham Evening Post*, Monday 8th June 1885.
16. *The Sheffield Daily Telegraph*, Tuesday 9th June 1885.
17. *The Sheffield Daily Telegraph*, Thursday 11th June 1885.
18. *The Sheffield Daily Telegraph*, Wednesday 17th June 1885.
19. *The Sheffield Weekly Telegraph*, Saturday 13th June 1885.
20. *The High Peak News*, Saturday 20th June 1885.
21. *The High Peak News*, Saturday 11th July 1885.
22. *The Derbyshire Times and Chesterfield Herald*,
      Saturday 27th February 1886.
23. *The Sheffield Daily Telegraph*, Friday 26th February 1886.
24. *The Sheffield and Rotherham Independent*,
      Tuesday 23rd February 1886.
25. *The Nottingham Evening Post*, Monday 6th May 1889.
26. *The Sheffield Daily Telegraph*, Monday 8th June 1885.

KILLED FOR THREEPENCE

JOHN MASSEY, DALBURY,
MONDAY APRIL 25TH 1910

ld John Massey of Dalbury died a violent death that came upon him unexpectedly. Maybe it could have been predicted, however, for although he was a normally friendly man by all accounts, being described as being 'naturally of a genial disposition' (1), he had a dislike for tramps and others of their ilk whom he saw as lazy scoundrels, and he wasn't slow to tell them so. It could be that this was the trigger that led to his murder.

John worked the Rook Hills Farm in Dalbury Parish, which lies in the countryside, six miles west of Derby. The old man had previously farmed at Osmaston and Tideswell. After thirty years he had finally handed Rook Hills over to his son John Massey junior four years previously and moved to White House at Dalbury Hollow. It was an isolated place that stood on the four lane ends where the road from Derby to the small village of Dalbury crossed the road from Etwall to the larger village of Dalbury Lees, two miles north. Though John had officially retired as a farmer and didn't need to work, being quite wealthy, he was very active and healthy for his 72 years of age. He had a large garden he worked in, and he kept poultry and a couple of milk cows in an old barn just up the road near to his house, besides working at times on his son's farm. His wife had died the previous November, but he had a housekeeper, Marian Salisbury, who had been with the family for five years since she was thirteen years old, working as a domestic servant. John was a spry old fellow who walked with a stoop and had a very discernible broken nose from an accident many years before. He was very well-known in the area, being chairman of the local Conservative Party, a frequent church-goer, and had been in the past an overseer at Burton upon Trent Union, which provided for the poor of the area by way of a workhouse and parish relief. He had been a collector of the Poor Rate taxes in the parish of Dalbury, and also exhibited in local horticultural shows. Everyone knew John Massey, even in town, where he could often be seen doing business in the Old Cattle Market near the centre of Derby on market days, or having a sociable drink in the company of other farmers in the Corporation Hotel nearby.

Quite a few people in Derby knew Amos Peel and his brother-in-law John Dugan (Dougan or Duggin in some reports) as well – but for different reasons. Married to two sisters from Staffordshire, they gave their address as number 5, Wright Street in the old West End, a tough, working class area of the town. Number 5 was better known as Hitchman's, a common lodging house, and to the modern ear this may sound like a bed and breakfast, or 'digs', but in reality was a much lower category of residence. Sometimes called 'the poor man's hotel', more often 'a doss-house', a common lodging house was only one step up from the workhouse, as in the lodging-houses no task was required to be done in exchange for a night's stay. In 1910, around fourpence (2p) bought one a bed for the night, often to be shared with a stranger. Open dormitories for single sexes were common. Licenced by the local authority, lodging-houses were where the poorest in society drifted to as they struggled to survive.

Peel and Dugan were known as occasional rag-gatherers, pedlars of trifles on the streets, such as fly-papers or cheap toys, and often went begging from door to door to buy the next drink. They were quite able-bodied, Peel being 35 years old and Dugan 31, and Dugan was an ex-soldier.

On the morning of old John Massey's last day on earth, Peel and Dugan went up Ashbourne Road to 'try and get a few coppers (pennies) before going out with their cart', (2) as Peel later testified in court. They "sang" (begging slang for spun a fictitious tale to people) a couple of streets, got twopence, and then 'a gentleman gave them sixpence'. (2) They took that money straight into the Travellers Rest, bought two halves of beer 'and a packet of fags', then they 'decided to go into the country and do a day's begging.' (2) Their purpose seems to have been fairly obvious to all – a day's drinking at other people's expense: 'Villagers declare that the men, who were of the typical tramp class, became abusive when refused help, and that one, when offered bread, asked for money.' (3)

Reaching Kirk Langley they entered Mr. John Land's licensed premises and had half a pint of beer each. They probably begged around there for a while, for they came back two hours later and had more beer. That afternoon Mr. Land passed through Dalbury Lees and saw the same two men going to the door of a house at Dalbury Lees. It would seem that their intention was to work their way in a rough loop that ran anti-clockwise, pulling in the Dalbury Lees area and then Dalbury, then back past Dalbury Hollow where Massey lived, and on from there back to Derby.

One of the first people they approached in the Dalbury Lees area was a postman. They seemed to be quite menacing in their method of begging, for they stopped him and, he claimed, demanded money, and only let him go when he told them he had none. A witness saw them from a distance and described one as wearing blue overalls such as mechanics wore, and the other wearing a peaked cap. At about a quarter to three, they were in the Black Cow (now called The Cow) at Dalbury Lees, where they had some beer and bought a packet of Woodbines (cheap cigarettes). Around three o'clock they were begging in the village, and went to the door of Elizabeth Ann Mellor, where they spun a tale about being out of work and having walked from Crewe. They asked for money, but she said she had none. Peel asked for water and she gave them a drink. Peel drank some of it and offered it to his companion, but Dugan was angry and said, "I don't want any of that —— stuff," and threw it away. (4) (Dugan does seem to have been the most aggressive of the two men, as we shall see.) As they walked away, she heard them 'grumbling all the way until they got out of hearing, one of them saying "This is a nice —— road to come down and never get nothing." ' (5)

At ten minutes past three they begged a halfpenny off John Maddocks, a roadman, 'to make up the price of a pint of ale'. (4) He was working on the road between Dalbury and Dalbury Lees where the footpath left the main road and went to Trusley, He gave them a penny. They had already begged at several houses in the area and asked him for directions to the nearest public house and how far it was. He told them the nearest pub was at Sutton, and the shortest way was by the public footpath. By 3.40 pm they were beyond Dalbury, heading away from Derby, in the Trusley area. There they stopped a woman called Alice Tunnicliffe and asked directions to Trusley Manor, home of Major General Coke, a retired army officer, a veteran of the Boer War, and a Deputy Lieutenant of Derbyshire. Dugan told the woman he had served under Coke in the army, and as they were leaving, she heard him say to Peel, 'We must get money.' (4)

By 4 pm the pair were at Trusley Manor, where they were given some bread and meat and sixpence by the butler, and, they later claimed, threepence from the coachman, and left there at 4.10 pm. The butler later testified that he could walk from the house to John Massey's place in fifteen minutes. They had, seemingly, changed direction and were now heading back towards Derby and home, not heading for Sutton and the pub as they had earlier planned. A woman called Jane Brassington, who had been to see her sister at Rook Hills Farm with her baby, saw them walking along Trusley Road shortly after, heading in the direction of John Massey's house and cow shed, 'walking at a good rate.' (4) She later testified that she felt afraid of the men as she pushed her baby carriage towards home. They stared at her, and she thought them "nasty-looking." ' (4) Asked in court by the defence if she still found them nasty-looking she said she was 'troubled because they stared at her so hard when she met them in the country.' (4) They did strike several people as menacing; maybe that was how they 'sang the song' when they went begging together. Jane Brassington hurried on, and the couple of beggars drew closer to the White House, still walking fast, towards the vicinity of the cowshed that belonged to Massey.

*   *   *   *   *

John Massey had been busy all day. He had worked in his house in the morning, helping to load a piano for transportation to his daughter at Trowell, then in the afternoon he walked over to Rooks Hill farm to leave some letters with his daughter-in-law Bessie. After that he had stayed on his son's farm and worked alone on

The White House, Dalbury Hollow, where John Massey lived and died.
His cowshed where he was attacked was over the road

some fencing. He returned home about four o'clock, pausing to take his two cows to the barn some four hundred yards or so away from his house, and tie them up ready to be milked. He took a light tea with his servant, Marian Salisbury, then, as he owed her ninepence for some purchase she had made, he took his purse, a yellow canvas-type cloth bag, from his right hand trouser pocket and paid her a shilling and she gave him three pennies in return. She heard the coins chink in his bag but could not say whether he had any more money in the bag, which she saw him put back in his trouser pocket. John then picked up two milking pails and set off. He was a fast milker, his son said, and would have finished the whole operation in about ten minutes. The time must have been around four-thirty in the afternoon.

Half an hour later Marian went to collect eggs from the hen house near the cowshed, and there she saw John Massey, leaning against the centre door to the barn. His head and hands were covered in blood and he held one hand to his head. Marian '…asked him what had happened, but he could not speak.

However, he made a sign, putting his hand to his mouth and making an effort to utter something.' (1) Marian turned and ran across the fields to Rooks Hill Farm and told John's daughter in law Bertha 'Master has been kicked by a cow.' (5) Bertha came running, along with her husband, John Massey's son, John Jr.

By the time that they reached him, old John had collapsed back into the shed and was lying huddled on the floor. His son said, "Whatever is the matter with you, Dad? Which cow has kicked you?" (4) but the old man couldn't speak. He appeared to John Jr. to be pleased to see him, but he seemed distressed and was trying to tell his son something. One pail of milk with about three or four pints in it was by the door to the barn, showing he had milked one cow, and the other was still empty and in place, while the milking stool lay on its side on the ground inside the barn. Massey's keys and cap were found against the back wall, behind the cows. 'There was a good deal of blood near to the cap,' (1) John Jr. noticed, and Marian Salisbury said that 'on the inside (of the cap) there was a good deal of blood'. (1)

John was placed in a chair. His clothes were covered in dirt from the floor and were wet with his blood. There was blood on his forehead from a deep cut , his left eye was bruised and swollen, and later, when he had been carried back to his house and he was given brandy and his wounds were washed it was discovered that he had several bruises to his body, especially around the thighs. His right hand was cut to the bone across the second finger, and his right-hand trouser pocket had been cut both across and down. It was obvious that he had been holding onto his purse when the cuts were inflicted, and the cloth bag he used as a purse was missing. It was never found. It seemed that he had been punched in the eye and then knocked down by a blow over the head from something heavy, such as the milking stool, (maybe he had brandished it when he was surprised in the shed) and had put his hand in his pocket to save his money from being stolen. Once he had fallen to the floor someone had kicked him several times and when he wouldn't release his grip on his money, they had cut through the pocket and taken his purse, slashing John's hand open in the process. It had probably been harder for the attacker or attackers to get to John's money as he had a definite stoop, and so would have been semi-curled over on the floor between the cows and the wall while they were trying to get it. Possibly they cut through the pocket because it may have been dimly lit in the shed and in their haste they couldn't see what they were doing. His keys lay on the ground, but his pocket knife, which his housekeeper said he kept in his right hand pocket along with his keys and purse, was never found.

Both in the shed and at home, John kept indicating his pocket with his hands and at some stage John thought he wanted his keys, and replaced them in his pocket, but John continued to make signs. Obviously, he was trying to say he had been robbed of his money.

Dr. Minchin from Etwall was sent for and arrived around six that evening. He found John Massey in bed, being supported by his son. He examined the wounds, finding the main one to be a star-shaped wound above the middle of the forehead. He dressed the wounds and while he was doing this the old man, who was in a semi-conscious condition, partially raised himself several times. The doctor left the house at seven, having given instructions to the family on how to treat the old man, who was obviously in a serious condition. By eight o'clock John Massey died, without regaining the power of speech before he passed.

*　　*　　*　　*　　*

The police were notified, and around midnight, 'acting on information received', as it was termed at the inquest, Detective Inspector David Davis set out from Derby and arrived at the White House in the early hours of the morning. He viewed the body in an upper bedroom, and from witnesses interviewed was given a description of Peel and Dugan, which was transmitted to both County and Derby police forces. The hunt was on.

But what of Peel and Dugan? Where were they after 4.30 pm, the approximate time when John Massey went out to milk his cows and was so viciously attacked? For some reason, although they had been heading for Derby and home, relatively empty handed, after drinking the day's meagre takings, they turned round, and headed in the opposite direction, away from Derby. At a quarter to five, it was first reported, they begged at Goldhurst Farm at nearby Sutton on the Hill. Edith Woodward, the wife of the tenant farmer later testified at the inquest that Peel asked for assistance but was declined. She said that Peel talked very fast and said, ominously, that 'they were sorry to trouble her, but they must get away.' (6) Dugan hung back and did not speak. They begged again at around five o'clock from Charles Hibbs, at a farm in Long Lane, getting no money, but some bread and cheese. After that they disappeared from the area.

The police, not yet aware of the identity of the main suspects, thought that the pair might have headed for Burton-upon-Trent, but in fact they headed south, to Tutbury. There they stayed the night in a cheap lodging house, paying sixpence each for a bed for the night, and buying a pint of 'fourpenny' (a fairly weak, cheap ale). They didn't have enough money for food, and the landlady testified that they had only twopence left between them after they had paid her. Staying away from home was something they had never done before, and both Ruth Peel and Susannah Dugan, the men's wives, after searching for their husbands on Monday night, went in some distress to the police station and asked Inspector David Davies if the police had any knowledge of their husbands' whereabouts.

On the following morning, Tuesday, April 26th, Peel and Dugan left their night's lodging in Monk Street and left Tutbury, not heading for home, as might be supposed, but intending to head for Ashbourne, as will be shown later. By ten thirty a.m. they were a mile away in the Railway Tavern at Hatton where the landlord said they had a pint of beer and asked him for a sheet of writing paper and envelope. They told him a variation of the story they had been using yesterday when begging: that they were workmen who had walked from Crewe looking for work in Derby (sometimes they said they were on their way back to Crewe, having found there was no work in Derby). They said they wanted to write and let their wives know where they were. A sympathetic man in the tap room gave them a stamp. Peel wrote the letter, then handed it to Dugan to read. He was heard to say, "That will do," and whisper something that couldn't be discerned. Peel then placed it in his pocket, and the landlord noticed that Peel had not written an address on the envelope. (7)

If the pair hoped to evade detection they were soon sadly

disappointed; as they approached the crossroads in Hatton, Police Constable Moore, who was in plain clothes at the time, espied the scruffy couple of men and cycled up to them. Giving evidence later, he said that when he approached them, they were eating bread and cheese, which was contained in a large handkerchief, and Peel also carried some sort of bundle under his arm. He stopped and asked where they came from (he later denied, when questioned in court by one of the men that he opened by saying "What's your little game? What game have you two been on with?" (8), but it seems too good not to be true!). Peel 'sang the song' about the long walk from Crewe to Derby once more, saying they were heading back to Crewe, but it was not to be. The constable had a written description of the two men seen in the Dalbury area on the previous day. He took it from his pocket and having compared it with Peel and Dugan told them he 'was going to arrest them on suspicion of murder at Dalbury the previous day. The short man (Dugan) replied, "Don't you think I can read that backwards; we know nought about it."(1) Later Peel and Dugan denied that the constable had mentioned murder at all when first arresting them. He said, they claimed, merely, ' "You are wanted in the Derby district." ' (8) A bobby of the olden times was not above bending police procedure and even the law to suit his need, and when Moore apprehended the men, he was on his own. Perhaps he thought to give the impression they were wanted on some minor charge, and once they were safe in the cell at his station house, he could then hand them over to Derby to interrogate and charge. Dugan maintained at the hearing before the magistrates that ' "You (P.C. Moore) never mentioned the word murder until after we were in the police station. So we naturally though it was only a case of begging." ' (8)

The constable seems to have been a little remiss in not cuffing the men, merely escorting them back towards the police station he occupied. When the party reached the crossroads, he told them to turn left towards his station, and Peel replied, "We are not going to go. You will have to fight for it," (1) and they both ran away from him, in the direction of Derby. Moore shouted to a roadman in front of them, called Whiting, to stop them. He was armed with a heavy roadbrush, and barred their way, so they turned and ran back toward P.C. Moore, veering to the right, up Malthouse Lane, which ran between open fields. Moore pursued them on his bicycle, detained Peel and handcuffed him. He gave him to Whiting to detain, and cycled on after Dugan, who took to the fields to evade the policeman. Moore merely watched which way he went, cycled round and hid in a ditch until Dugan came near. Jumping a gate, Moore easily caught up with a winded Dugan, but he would not give up without a fight. He said to the policeman, obviously referring to his army service, "I have stopped bullets, and you'll have to fight for it." (1) He struck Moore in the chest, then drew back and ran at the policeman with his head down, trying to butt him, so Moore drew his truncheon and gave the man a couple of blows to the head and one on his left arm. Dugan soon changed his tune, shouting, "I give in," and then, when restrained, "Fetch a doctor." Then, very significantly, some would say, he asked Moore to 'hit him again on the head and finish him off.' (1) Whiting the roadman also testified that when he had blocked his way earlier, Dugan had asked him to hit him over the head with his heavy road brush. Considering that only the day before they had been in the area where an old man had been killed by a blow to the head, those two requests seem very significant.

Even more incriminating is a comment Amos Peel made to Whiting as they stood and watched P.C. Moore chase off after Dugan. He said, "I hope he will get him. It was he that did it. It would have been better for me if I hadn't shown fight." (1) What else could 'it' have been but the attack on John Massey? Further, Whiting said that Peel was 'trembling very much' when he said it. (9) One newspaper quotes Peel slightly differently, or it could have been more that he said whilst waiting for Moore to apprehend Dugan:

'Benjamin Whiting, a roadman, said that Peel told him that his companion was a fool, adding: He has made it worse for me. It is not me, it is him that has done it." ' (10)

If it really was the case, as they claimed in court, that they only thought they were being taken in for begging, why would Peel have told the roadman that it was Dugan who did 'it', and why were they both so desperate to escape? Why did Dugan even ask, somewhat melodramatically, for both the roadman and the constable to strike him over the head and kill him quickly? They may not have known that John Massey was dead and they would be charged with his murder, but they seemed to know they were wanted for something more petty than begging.

As Dugan refused to walk – Moore tried dragging him for some distance – a pony and trap was sent for and the two men were taken to Hatton Police Station and locked in the single cell there.

On the same morning that the two beggars were arrested, a post-mortem on John Massey was taking place at the White House, conducted by Dr. Minchin of Etwall. He noted that the deceased had a swollen 'black' left eye, most probably caused by a blow from a fist, numerous bruises on the thighs, likely to have been from kicks, and a deep cut, down to the bone, on the second finger of the right hand. Death had been as a result of a at least two blows from a heavy, blunt instrument such as the milking stool.

Dr. Minchin '…found a composite fracture of the skull, which had been broken into several pieces. There was also a fracture over the left ear, with a piece of bone hanging loose. There was another fracture across the top of the forehead, and another ran across the top of the head… Death was due to concussion of the brain caused by compound fracture.' (9)

* * * * *

The police had a body; they had the suspects; they had a motive; now they needed to keep the suspects in custody while an inquest made it official that a murder had occurred and who was most likely responsible, and a case for prosecution could be prepared. By five o'clock in the afternoon, Inspector Davies arrived and viewed the prisoners, then took them into his charge and they were escorted to Derby Police Office, where they were charged together on suspicion of the wilful murder of John Massey at Dalbury. Peel replied, "I will plead not guilty at present," and Dugan replied, "I will say the same." (9)

Not guilty, at present. This is quite a curious thing for both to say, given that subsequently they vehemently denied anything to do with the murder and swore they were never anywhere near Massey's cowshed. It is tantamount to saying that they could be guilty, and it is noteworthy that it is Peel who says it first, after recently implying that it was Dugan who killed Massey. Peel seems to be saying he is not guilty but might plead otherwise if offered some sort of lesser charge, such as being an accessory to the crime, which would not carry the death penalty.

On Wednesday 27th April, a preliminary inquest was held at John Massey's house. The coroner said he did not intend to do more than take evidence of identity of the deceased at present, while further evidence was prepared to lay before the jury to enable them to reach a proper verdict. John Massey Jr., who broke down when he spoke of the condition he found his father in, gave evidence, saying also that at first they had all thought it to be a kick from a cow that had caused his father's injuries, and it was only when they discovered his father's purse missing as the old man had repeatedly tried to tell them, although struck dumb by the attack and reduced to gestures, that they realised he had been violently attacked. The coroner said a post-mortem examination had been made and would be heard at the resumed inquiry. The inquest was then adjourned for a week.

On the same day, Peel and Dugan were remanded in custody until the Friday at a brief appearance before magistrates, while police continued to gather evidence.

By the Friday, when they were brought by police before a magistrates' court to apply for a further remand, Peel had obviously had time to rethink his gaffe, and when the magistrate asked prisoners if they had any questions of Inspector Davies, Peel asked if he was sure that was what Peel had said, claiming that he had actually said, "I will plead not guilty of the charge." Davies held firm however and affirmed that he had reported accurately what Peel and Dugan had said. (Ironically, one of the magistrates on the bench was Major-General Talbot Coke, whom Dugan claimed while begging on the day of the murder to have served under.) They were remanded in custody for a further week. It was clear there were no other suspects, and the remands would stretch out until the Quarter Assizes.

On the Saturday old John Massey was laid to rest, with a large number of mourners from the area attending. John had been a well-respected man, and it seemed the whole community had turned out to pay their respects, the small church being packed with relatives and friends, and a huge number of wreaths on the coffin and at the graveside. On the Sunday too there was a special service, and the vicar spoke of an almost-prophetic letter which John Massey had recently written to a friend who had been bereaved, quoting from it: "As the Scriptures say, we never know what a day may bring forth." (6) The murder was the sensation of Derby and district, as shown by the number of morbid visitors on the Sunday to the usually quiet little hamlet of Dalbury and the White House where the murder took place:

'During the day the site of the tragedy was visited by hundreds of people who came on foot, cycles, and conveyances, and many expressions of sympathy were heard from the visitors.' (6)

News of the sensational murder found its way in regional papers to the entire British Isles and even Southern Ireland, and the nationals reported it too. Perhaps the strangest headline when reporting it came from the *Belper News and Derbyshire Telephone* of April 29th, which somewhat tastelessly ran the report under the banner, 'Farmer Hammered In His Own Cowshed.' This is most likely to have been a reference to the old cottage trade in Belper of nail-making, and the tradition amongst the 'nailers' of taking their little nail-making hammers out with them as a fighting weapon when they went drinking, tucked into their belts.

The following Wednesday, May 4th, the resumed inquest was held. As there was no suitable building near to the White House, and Massey's house could not contain the number of witnesses called, along with jury and observers, police etc, it was held at Dalbury Lees in the schoolroom, and the children given a day off. Even the prisoners were brought to the inquest, with special seating in the schoolroom provided for them, and two warders accompanying. Strangely, the route taken to the inquest in the carriage from Derby Gaol to the schoolhouse was past the scene of the murder. Both prisoners later denied ever seeing the place before.

The inquest was fairly straightforward. John Massey Jr.'s statement was read over to the jury once more, then a succession of witnesses were called to either give evidence of John Massey senior's movements that day, or to speak of their sightings and meetings with the prisoners on the day of the murder. Dr. Minchin gave his report on the post-mortem examination, and was questioned by the Coroner quite closely as to whether it could have been an unfortunate accident, caused by a kick from a cow.

'The Coroner: could such a fracture be caused by a kick from a cow? Witness (Dr. Minchin): I think it would be very unlikely, in fact practically impossible. In reply to a question as to whether such an instrument as the milk stool (produced) would cause the injuries, witness said he should say that would be the thing which would cause the injuries. – The Coroner: Would they be caused by anything blunt? No, a heavy instrument would be capable of causing them. Witness added that kicks from a cow would cause more external wounds. The internal injuries were so severe, and a cow would have injured the external tissues far more severely. The large star-shaped wound on the head had no corresponding fracture directly beneath it, so that the injury causing the fractures must have been caused by a heavy smooth instrument, with a substance covering the head, such as a cap. The cap doubtless saved the skull from more external injuries – Supt. Richardson inquired whether the doctor thought the injury to the left eye was caused by a blow, or was it in sympathy with the fracture of the skull? I should say it would be caused by a blow. – Supt. Richardson: Might such an injury have been caused by a man's fist? Yes. – could the deceased have spoken after these injuries? I should say probably not at all. Certainly not within half-an-hour. – Assuming that the injuries were caused by a blow, can you say how many blows were struck? I should say that probably two blows were sufficient. – Would they have been one in the left eye and one on the top of the head? That is so.' (6)

Clearly it was believed by the police and others present that Peel and Dugan had followed Massey into his cowshed, possibly seeing him from a distance; he had reacted badly to their rather belligerent, even menacing, way of soliciting alms, and had told them to be on their way. Dugan being the more belligerent of the pair had probably taken the lead in attacking the old man, hitting him in the eye, and then crushing his skull with the milking stool, probably kicking him in the thigh while on the floor, maybe to try and get him to roll over, seeing that Massey had his hand firmly in his right pocket where his purse was. They had emptied his right pocket of his keys and a knife. The keys were found on the floor of the cowshed later; the knife was never found. We know John Massey was a shortish man with a pronounced stoop, and in such a confined space, up against the shed wall with two cows in the way, it must have been hard to rob the farmer as he lay on the floor. One of the men could have snatched up the knife and cut at the pocket, slashing Massey's finger to the bone as he did so.

At first there had been some confusion as to how much money Massey had on him when he went out to milk his cows. His son-in-law, John Bainbridge (or Bainbrigge, or Bembridge, or even Banbury, depending on the newspaper), had been with him on the Friday before, in the Corporation Hotel at Derby, and saw John Massey had seven or eight gold sovereigns when he had opened his purse and paid the younger man a debt of some twenty five shillings, 'and on the Saturday had heard a rattle suggesting that the money was still in the purse.' (11) Subsequently, though, five pounds was found in John's desk at the White House, so it would seem that, after market day, with stock being bought and sold at auction, supplies ordered and paid, deals even struck in the hotel bar, John put his money somewhere safe and carried only small change. It wouldn't have been wise, or necessary, to be carrying large sums of money on his person while working out in the field or barn, as he had been doing that day, so it would be quite possible – indeed most likely – that all John had in his purse when robbed were the three pennies Marion the housekeeper had given him in change for a shilling earlier. Threepence for his life serves to highlight the stupidity and brute savagery of the crime, as well as a random act of opportunism, committed by a person or persons who were strangers to John Massey.

Having established how Massey had died, the inquest needed to ascertain, if possible, who was responsible, and enough witnesses came forward to show that Peel and Dugan were in the vicinity of the cowshed at the time of Massey''s death, if not actually there. Mr. John White, the County Analyst gave evidence on testing the clothes of the prisoners for blood, finding none, he said, on the actual outer clothes, but on the large kerchief Peel had with him, he found a fresh blood smear of mammalian blood, about two inches long that was less than a week old, and he had yet to conduct more tests. Also significant was the fact that the left sleeve of Peel's shirt had been torn off completely and was missing, and the threads at the edge of the tear appeared new. There were small bloodstains on the shirts of both men, and the analyst declared that they appeared to all be of the same age as the stain on the kerchief.

The Coroner summed up eventually, saying that the inquest had been a long one, over six hours in all, but it had been necessary to give the jury sufficient evidence to reach a verdict. He stressed to the jury that to show that the two men 'being in the Dalbury Lees district was not sufficient to warrant their conviction of the crime. Before a jury found them guilty they must have evidence of such a nature as would leave no doubt that they were the men who inflicted the terrible injuries on the unfortunate man.' (6) The jury thought they had enough, for after a brief ten minutes they delivered the verdict 'That John Massey was wilfully murdered by Amos Peel and John Dugan.' (6)

Two days later, on Friday May 6th the prisoners were brought to magistrates court for further remand. As usual in these cases, a large crowd had assembled to see them brought in. The court was close to the West End of Derby, where they lived, and their wives were to the fore, with many friends and neighbours, plus the usual morbidly curious. Inside the courtroom their wives sat, and as Peel and Duggan were brought through: 'A woman in the front of the court cried out, "Amos, keep your mouth shut!" She was immediately silenced, and the men appeared to take no notice of the remark.' (12) It would have been impossible, though, not to hear it, and the intention was obvious. Peel had said enough already to make both he and Dugan appear guilty of more than a vagrancy charge and could get them hanged if he were to say more.

On the next remand, however, further sensation was caused in court when the contents of the letter Peel had written on the morning shortly before their arrest, in the Railway Tavern at Hatton was read out. The letter had been found concealed behind some hot water pipes when Mrs. Moore had cleaned the cell after the prisoners had been removed to Derby. It was meant for the prisoners' wives, and read:

'Dear Wives, Just these few lines to let you know we are all right after getting locked up at Hatton, and are glad to say that we got clinched (some reports say "chucked", but the meaning is to be taken as "released" or "freed") this morning by the skin of our teeth, but having nothing to return home with we decided to keep away. We hope to see you both at Ashbourne on Wednesday afternoon all being well. Please take back the cart, and also get the papers from Hannah, and oblige, Jack and Amos.' (11)

Bearing in mind that in those days there were usually several collections of mail and a message sent in one postal area was usually delivered on the same day, it seems Peel and Dugan expected their wives to know within a few hours on Tuesday that they weren't returning home. The discovery and contents of the letter throws a strong suspicion on the men, and several points are worth examining here.

First, when the letter was written that morning in the pub at Hatton Peel had not put the address on the envelope. Was this because they were afraid of the address being seen in the pub and passed on to the police if they came asking about them?

Secondly, there was no public lockup where vagrants were held overnight, as they claimed in their letter. By this date the old village lockups were not used, and the police didn't lock vagrants up overnight at Hatton, according to the papers of the time. Their purpose in telling their wives they had been restrained by the law overnight seems to be, probably, to keep secret the reason that they were intending not to return home: that they had attacked a farmer, and might be looked for at their home address, nor would they want the neighbours back home, or anyone intercepting the letter, maybe, to know what had really happened to keep them away from home.

Thirdly, they told their wives to meet them at Ashbourne on the following day, and this suggests they were going to disappear from Derbyshire, possibly going across the county border into Staffordshire, where their wives were from, or even further, maybe to Dumfries, where they had all been recently. A cart was to be returned, papers brought to Ashbourne with them, though these papers aren't explained, but obviously important to one of the men.

Could they have been army records for John Dugan, perhaps his papers of discharge? Was he, perhaps, in receipt of army pension and they had been left with Hannah (maybe their landlady) for surety? The *Nottingham Evening News* (13) reported that Dugan was indeed in receipt of an army pension, so perhaps they were related to this. Could they have been vital evidence as to their identity if the police went to Hutchins' Lodging House on Wright Street, and Hannah, whoever she was, handed them over? We shall never know, but this detail in the letter does seem to be suggesting that the wives clear up any evidence and leave the lodging house – and Derby – quickly.

The final point is that the prisoners did not want the letter found and did their best to hide it. If it was an innocent letter, why conceal it?

*   *   *   *   *

The trial of Peel and Dugan opened at the County Hall on Wednesday 29th of June before Mr. Justice Lawrence. The case had excited great local interest, and as a result the public thronged the courtroom and there was a large crowd in the concourse before the County Hall in St. Mary's Gate. Promptly at 10.30 a.m. the accused were called and ran up the steps to the dock and faced the judge. Peel was dressed in a blue serge suit with a low collar and red tie, while Dugan was described as wearing a dark reefer suit with a dirty green kerchief about his neck. They pleaded not guilty 'in clear and emphatic voices' (14) and then were seated.

Appearing for the prosecution were Ryland Adkins K.C., M.P., and Mr. Howard d'Eggville. For the defence was Mr. Lipson Ward, a young barrister who was showing much promise. This was his first case of any importance and he was determined to put up a good fight in what seemed a fairly open-and-shut case, judging by the newspapers of the time. Only twenty-nine years old, he prepared for the two days of the time with thoroughness, knew his brief inside out, and produced in court visual aids such as maps to make his points to the jury. He was an excellent speaker, persuasive, and 'speaking with a quiet, convincing eloquence...' (15)

The trial was to last only two days, mainly because there was a lack of detailed evidence to present, and this was obviously a problem for the prosecution. It seems they had a sufficiency of circumstantial evidence, but no direct evidence that would place the two wandering ragmen in that cowshed and provide a witness who saw them attack John Massey. They could only say that the two men were in the Dalbury area, in need of money, and became truculent and aggressive when denied it. There were bloodstains, but these could not be proven, in the early days of forensics, to be human blood, let alone belong to the victim. They had a difficult job. There was other, circumstantial evidence too, however, that the defence needed to either explain away or circumvent by ignoring it if the prosecution did not make too much of it, and by and large the prosecution does not seem to have distinguished itself.

On the first day the prosecution opened the case to the jury and recounted the death of John Massey. Witnesses testified as to the whereabouts of Massey, and to his injuries, and other witnesses spoke to times and whereabouts of Peel and Dugan and to their doings in Tutbury and Hatton, and their eventual arrest. Lipson could not argue with any of this, but when John Massey Jr. testified to coming to White Hills and finding his father badly wounded and bleeding, the defence lawyer, in cross-examination, attempted to sow a little seed of doubt in the jury's mind. Massey Jr. had a man in his employ at the time who was later prosecuted for extreme cruelty to a horse, hadn't he? he asked, and went into some gory detail about it. Massey admitted it to be true, and Lipson asked if the man was still in prison for the offence. Massey said yes, and Lipson asked where that man was when old Massey was in his cowshed. Massey Jr. replied that he was milking with the other farm labourers at Rooks Hill Farm, and stayed there, was there when he got back, and it was he who had been sent for the doctor to come, but it must have brought home to the jury that there were other people in the area who were capable of cold-blooded deeds. It seemed barely relevant, and maybe a sterner judge would have reproved the counsel, but it left in the jury's minds that it need not have been an outsider who had done such an awful thing as to kill the old man.

Regarding the milking stool being used as the murder weapon,

Massey Jr. testified that he had occasion to look at the stool on the morning of his father's murder, as he thought to use it as a seat in a float. It had a crack in it, he had noticed, that had been closed up with a peg, but after his father's murder he saw that the crack was gaping as if it had been struck against something. Asked about his father's attitude to beggars by the prosecution, 'What sort of a temper would he be likely to display towards tramps?' Massey Jr. replied, 'He would be rather hasty.' (16)

Lipson Ward asked about the purse, and if someone among the local people who came to the scene of the attack to help, could have picked it up, but Massey said he searched the shed before anyone came and was sure it was not there then.

That concluded the case for the prosecution and now came the chance for Lipson Ward to refute what looked like a damning case against his clients. One of his tactics in cross-examination had been to chip away at the circumstantial evidence in the case, even spread some confusion, showing the jury that there was more than one interpretation to be placed on some evidence. He even tried to explore during cross examination of Doctor Minchin the possibility that one of Massey's cows had kicked the old man when he bent over to pick the stool up, and that may have caused the injury. Quite how the cow might have slashed open Massey's pocket and stolen his purse he didn't get far enough to suggest, as the doctor quashed the idea of the cow having kicked John Massey quite decisively.

* * * * *

Intense excitement was generated in the packed courtroom when the first defence witnesses were called; they were the accused, Peel and Dugan. It is generally considered risky to put up the defendant in a case such as this, as it opens them to cross-examination, but Ward was very confident in his conduct and must have considered that without the presence of direct evidence they had killed Massey, and with his clients well-briefed, he was safe.

Peel came first. He was nervous and found the case hard to follow. He testified that he was a native of Long Eaton, a Derbyshire town some ten miles away, a centre of lace making. He gave an exhaustive account of his and Dugan's day, places called at and the times. He detailed conversations with prosecution witnesses and said that the missing time when Massey was murdered, when no one could account for them, was occupied with eating bread and cheese they had been given. They had a smoke and decided to go on an extended begging tour to Uttoxeter, though he never explained why they didn't go there, and didn't explain why they instead stayed overnight at Tutbury then came back and headed for Ashbourne. The closest they had come to Massey's house was when they turned at the corner of the nearest field and headed back to Goldhurst Farm. His shirt had blood on it from sorting rabbit skins, he claimed, and the missing piece of his shirt he had torn off in Dumfries some five weeks before when it got in the way while he was washing overalls. Lipson Ward then took Peel to the next day and his arrest, and he claimed that he thought he was going to be arrested for begging as he had just been up to some houses in Hatton and had some bread and cheese under his coat. He claimed that the policeman, Constable Moore, did not tell he and Dugan that they were wanted on suspicion of murder and he further said that they had been an hour in the lockup before they overheard the allegation of murder and immediately knocked on the cell door and gave their names in, which they had refused to do earlier. Both prisoners had testified earlier that the policeman had, understandably perhaps, when facing two potential murderers on his own, lied to them by saying, 'I only want you to come with me while I telephone. You will not be detained long.' (1) Asked if he had killed the old man, Peel replied that 'I never saw him, let alone kill him. I could not tell you where the shed is yet, only from what I have heard.' (17)

When Mr. Adkins got up to cross-examine Peel, he observed that Peel was 'not a bad hand at making up stories,' to which Peel replied that he 'was the same as anyone else.' (17)

"I'm not so sure of that. You know how to make up a story if it is useful or likely to be useful,"(17) Adkins replied, but he could not shake or trap Peel into a discernible lie.

He moved on to question Peel closely as to how much they had spent in public houses whilst out on their begging. Peel said they had spent one shilling and fivepence (about 7p) on the day of the murder, and ninepence (just under 4p) on the morning of their arrest:

'As to the 1s 5d (7p), he received 6d (2½p) of this from the butler at Trusley Manor, 6d from the parson at Sutton, and 3d (1¼p) from his coachman, apart from odd pennies received.

'Mr Adkins: "And threepence from old Mr. Massey in the cowshed?" ' (17)

One can almost hear the contempt in that last question, and, incredibly, Peel said yes to it, then, when Adkins repeated the question slightly louder, he denied it strongly, saying he was never near the cowshed.

Peel also denied that Whiting had heard him say that it was Dugan who had done 'it' and that he (Peel) was innocent, saying that Whiting had 'misjudged' him. He was also asked to explain why the threads on the end of the bloodstained torn shirt, a shirt he claimed to have torn seven weeks previously, were new, he denied that they could be described as new.

Adkins asked as he wound up his cross-examination, 'how are we to tell today that the story you tell now is not untrue, like all those others you have told?' and Peel replied, 'I have sworn before God that I would speak the truth.' (17)

Adkins tried one last time with him, saying, more for the jury than Peel, 'Did you not, after passing Mrs. Brassington, go across that field and find this old man in his cowshed, quarrel with him and knock him down, cut his purse out of his pocket, and go away not knowing or caring what happened to him?' (17) Peel strongly denied it, as a man would whose life was on the line.

At this stage Inspector Davies was recalled to be examined as to a claim Peel had made that he had originally, at the first magistrates hearing, asked to be sworn and give evidence before the magistrates, and had been wrongly denied the opportunity. The Inspector said he didn't recall it happening and Lipson Ward asked Davies if it hadn't been reported in the *Derby Daily Telegraph*?' The Inspector said he did not know, and the Judge intervened, saying that question could not be asked. Re-examination can only be used to ask further questions about matters arising out of cross-examination and is usually used to clarify any matters defence cross-examined the witness about. Lipson Ward was widening the defence case at this point, it seemed, but it was possible to bring in the reporter from the newspaper to affirm that he had heard Peel ask for the chance to make a statement and give evidence under oath at the magistrates hearing, and that was being arranged as Dugan was brought to the stand.

Dugan walked to the witness box with almost a military bearing, shoulders back and confident, as he had done since he was first brought to the magistrates hearings. It is quite possible that for once Dugan was telling the truth when he said that he had been a soldier, and served under Major-General Talbot Coke, for he seems to have had a connection with Dumfries, and Talbot Coke commanded at one time the 3rd Battalion of the Kings Own Scottish Borderers, whose barracks were in that town until 1910, when they transferred to Berwick.

When Dugan was asked about the large silk handkerchief of his that bore bloodstains, he said that it was found in a pile of rags, and he explained that the blood on this and his shirt came about when an old lady in his house slipped and fell downstairs, damaging her ankle, and he had helped her upstairs, getting blood on his shirt in the process. He had wiped the blood away with his handkerchief. She had later died.

Looking at the inquest report we find that the old lady was a Sarah Lomas, and, like the Peels and the Dugans, she lived at the rather run-down and seedy lodging house, known as Hitchman's, number 5, Wright Street. The 'old lady' had slipped when she was assisted upstairs at ten-thirty on the evening of 22nd April when she had returned home being very much the worse for drink. Having taken Sarah Lomas upstairs and left her on the landing, Susannah Dugan had to go downstairs again to fetch the key to Sarah's room, the door being locked. The stairs were open on one side, except for the handrail, and on Susannah's return, she had found the drunken Sarah at the bottom of the stairs with a bloody wound to her head (no mention of the ankle!). Dugan himself had helped Susannah carry Sarah up to bed, and she had stayed there, abusive and refusing medical help for three days until she was removed to the Workhouse, where she died. Whether it was true that Dugan got blood on him then or not, it served to put doubt into the jury's mind: Sarah's or old John's – whose blood was it?

Mr Adkins said to Dugan, 'I put it to you that you went across to this cowshed, that you had plenty of beer in you, that you wanted money and attacked this old man, two of you, cut out his purse and left him knocked down in the corner of his shed.' Dugan replied, 'No sir. I never saw him.' (17) It was not meant that Dugan should answer in any other way; the charge was meant to register with the jury and sway their opinion.

This led Adkins on to Dugan's strange behaviour on the day following the murder, when apprehended at Hatton. He had asked Whiting the roadman to "Hit me on top of the head with that brush." To P.C. Moore, after he had hit him twice on the head with a truncheon after Dugan had attacked the officer, "Hit me again and finish me," and also to Moore, before being subdued, "I have faced bullets, and you will have to fight for it." (17) He denied making the first two statements and said that the last one 'Came into his head to say it, although he only thought he was being arrested for begging.' (17) It was a weak reply, but nothing was admitted. He may have said too much, earlier on in the case, but Dugan was guarding his mouth now.

Susannah Dugan was the next witness and bore out her husband's testimony regarding finding the handkerchief in a pile of rags, and her husband helping the old lady who fell downstairs. She also claimed that she had tried to wash the blood out of the handkerchief with cold water, with no success. Ruth Peel followed and gave evidence, and in cross-examination by Adkins admitted that it was unusual for her husband to stay out all night. Other witnesses followed for the defence but added nothing of importance.

A reporter for the *Derby Daily Telegraph*, who was in court, a Mr. John Piper, was called to show that Peel had asked at the first magistrates court after his arrest for the opportunity to give evidence under oath, and been denied. He had said that 'the time would be going on and he wished to be sworn to give evidence.' The magistrate had replied, incorrectly, that 'he could not do so at present, and the two men were marched back to the cells.' (18)

One cannot help but feel that an important chance was missed there. Peel wanted to 'give evidence', not merely to protest his innocence, but possibly to supply some sort of proof. Whatever he wanted to swear on oath was never explained, but it could be the reason that someone, at the next magistrates court, shouted out for Amos to 'keep his mouth shut.' Most likely it was Susannah Dugan, afraid of what Amos might say further, that he might become a witness against her husband, given that he already allegedly told Whiting that it was Dugan who did 'it'. Peel took the hint and never deviated from their story again. What might he have said further, in a bid to save his own skin? We shall never know, and all because of a magistrate wrongly versed in the law.

With Piper's evidence, that concluded the case for the defence, and the Crown recalled Mr. White, the County Analyst, to attest that if Mrs Dugan had attempted, as she had stated, to wash out the bloodstains on the handkerchief used by Dugan, the stains would have been obliterated, and that he was convinced that no attempt had been made to wash out the stains with warm water. In other words, the bloodstains were probably fresher than she was claiming, standing by his original testimony that the stains he had examined a few days after the men's arrest were less than a week old. White was also examined again by prosecuting counsel Mr. Adkins as to the tear in Peel's shirt sleeve and he gave it as his expert opinion that the tear was recent when he examined it, not five weeks old as Peel claimed. Peel also claimed that some small bloodstains further up the sleeve were the result of insects being crushed against his body when he was in Dumfries (either a flea or a bedbug?), but White disputed that also, saying the blood was on the exterior of the fabric and was also the wrong colour, being brown, not reddish. Basically, he had testified that both men had fresh, human bloodstains on their clothing, and one man, Peel, had recently torn a piece off his shirtsleeve. It was as far as he could go, given the limitations of forensic science in the early part of the last century.

The court adjourned for the day, leaving the defence and prosecution to make their final case the following day, to be followed by the judge's summing up and the jury's deliberation.

On the Thursday, Lipson Ward addressed the jury for the defence. Again he returned to the fact that the prosecution had nothing but circumstantial evidence, saying that 'the prosecution knew that theirs was a weak case, and they had done everything to prop it up.' (17) He tried to present the prisoners in a more sympathetic light than most people had viewed them, not threatening at all, just two men, almost jolly vagabonds by his description, who 'behaved quite peacefully to the many people from whom they begged.' (17) In the time shortly after Masson had been attacked by someone unknown, Lipson Ward claimed, the accused 'went quietly along, begging and talking to whom they met, and left a complete trail for anyone to follow.' (17) He chose to overlook the testimony of Mrs. Woodward, who said that when the two men showed up in her orchard at Goldhurst Farm, less than half an hour after the murder, Dugan hung back and Peel was so agitated by something that he spoke very fast, so that she could hardly understand what he was saying, and that he apologised, saying they must get away. It is worth noting here that this is the first known occasion that Peel asked if the person they begged from had an old shirt to spare. It had been five weeks, he later claimed, that he had been wearing a shirt with a sleeve missing, but it is only then that he thinks to beg for a replacement.

Lipson Ward bent the times and behaviour of the two men quite cynically in their defence. To make it impossible for them to have done the crime, he had to account for their time between leaving Trussley Manor, and the time they came to Goldhurst Farm, and to make the time at which Massey was fatally assaulted to be later than 4.30pm, as estimated by the time the farmer went to the shed, milked his first cow, and put the pail with milk in by the door. At first, he said, Marion Salisbury had told the magistrates that she and John Massey sat down to take tea at 4.15 pm, but the prosecution had corrected this to four o'clock, however, Lipson Ward said that 'the story told to the magistrates was likely to be the correct one, as it was told while the facts were fresher in the mind.' (17) That, conveniently for the defence, makes it a little later for Massey to reach the shed. Massey then milked the first cow (evidence had been given by Massey's son that the first cow was 'going off' so gave little milk and would take less time to milk), which Lipson Ward said, 'All that would take a few minutes. John Massey's son had said about three minutes, but he, counsel, was entitled to say in favour of the prisoners that it might have been a little longer!' (17) This is astounding, really. A privately-educated

Cambridge law graduate from a wealthy family feels that he can correct a man who has farmed all his life on how long it takes his own father to milk a cow! And what 'entitled' him? It was arrogant beyond measure, but cleverly done, and he got away with it.

Now, having moved the time for the attack to have been done closer to five o'clock, Lipson Ward looked at the time the two men arrived to beg at Goldhurst Farm. Originally, he said, the farmer's wife said the men came to her in the orchard about five o'clock, but her later evidence was that it was around a quarter to five, and 'counsel submitted this was probably more correct than the statement the previous day, that it was just about five o'clock.' (17) Here Lipson Ward doesn't argue that the first time given is likelier to be the correct one (as he did earlier when Marion Salisbury corrects her time) by arguing that it would be fresher in the mind, but just accepts a later time as 'probably more correct!' It was verbal sleight of hand, nothing more.

It is interesting here to note that time was a little 'elastic' in the country in those days. Most people did not possess watches, and clocks were often five or ten minutes fast or slow, before the advent of radio and regular time checks. No one thought, for example, to ask Mrs. Woodward whether she knew the time Peel and Dugan accosted her to be accurate, or was estimating it to be a quarter to five, no one asked Marion Salisbury whether there was a clock in the farmhouse that she set the time of Massey's departure by, and if so, was it generally accurate. Here the prosecution could have demolished Lipsom Ward's argument but did not raise it.

Given that Peel and Dugan 'dropped off the map' for about half an hour, at the same time as the murder, and were last seen by a Mrs. Brassington about a field away from Massey's cowshed just before the murder, how did the defence explain what they were doing in the time that there were no sightings of the men, no alibi provided? Lipson Ward said that 'after leaving Trusley Manor and hungry as they were, they sat down and ate the food they had begged. The probabilities were all in favour of this course.' (17) It could, of course just as well be a 'probability' that they were in Massey's cowshed, beating the old man to death and slashing him with a knife to get a mere threepence from him.

As to the bloodstains on the shirts of the men, defence said that it was not likely that the men had taken their coats off to attack Massey and rob him, but no stains were found on their coats. He also pointed out that witnesses (wives and a friend) testified to seeing the bloodstained handkerchief in the days before the murder. Most importantly, and finally, Lipson Ward stressed that the lives of the two accused rested on the decision of the jury, a weighty decision to make, whether two men should hang or not:

"The jury had to decide… whether two more lives were to be added to the one that had been lost in this terrible human tragedy. He asked them to say that the hands of the prisoners were not stained with John Massey's blood." (17)

Mr Adkins, for the Crown, pointed out that the men were out on a begging expedition, and drinking the proceeds as they went along, not seeming to have missed a public house on their route. Peel, he said, had stated at one point what was important: 'We must have money.' (17) He said that Peel's story was fluent until he came to the point where he had to explain the missing half hour, a time during which Massey was attacked and later died from the injuries received. He pointed out that at 4.20 pm they were within a field of the place where the cowshed stood, that Mr. Massey went to his cowshed about 4.30 pm, and that this 'could have been the very time that the prisoners came along the road leading to within a few yards of the cowshed. If the prisoners reached this place – as counsel submitted they did – and inflicted fatal injuries on Mr. Massey, all that was a matter of a very short time indeed. The doctor had said as much.' (17)

Adkins then pointed out that at this point in time, the prisoners, who had every intention of going home that night, never having stayed out at night before, and who were heading for Derby, suddenly turned and made off, away from Derby. If the prisoners, had injured Mr. Massey, he suggested, they would have every reason for getting away from the Derby district, and: 'Accordingly, they sent a letter to their wives to join them elsewhere, written in a way that would explain why they desired this, but giving no hint of what had actually happened.' (17) Their conduct after the crime showed growing fear, he said, and the 'extravagant' remarks made after apprehension, such as 'Hit me and finish me,' and 'Hit me over the head with that brush,' by Dugan, and 'I wish they had got him,' and 'He did it,' by Peel 'were not in keeping with the idea that begging was the allegation against them.' (17)

There Adkins closed his case, and it was now only left for the judge to sum up and the jury to deliberate and deliver a verdict.

*   *   *   *   *

The judge began by instructing the jury in what was the legal definition of manslaughter, the alternative verdict available to them, but warned against bringing that verdict in 'as a mere matter of shrinking from a verdict which the evidence they accepted might justify.' (17) It really turned on whether the death had been the result of a quarrel between the two parties or whether it had resulted from a joint act of robbery with violence. If they thought the prisoners had attacked John Massey with that intention, of taking his money, and he had died as a result, then that would be murder. On the other hand, if they had quarrelled and in the course of the quarrel a blow had been struck with a weapon which a reasonable man would not expect would prove fatal, then the jury could be justified in bringing in a verdict of manslaughter. Further, if the jury had any doubt about the case, then they should find the accused not guilty.

Regarding defence's claim that the evidence put forward by prosecution was circumstantial, his Lordship said that most evidence in murder cases was circumstantial, that murder 'was a crime not often committed in broad daylight.' (17) He then pointed out a very salient fact: at the time that the crime was committed the prisoners were in the area, and that no other persons were seen there. He commented, too, on the fact that the letter found in the cell at Hatton on the day after the murder showed that they intended to leave the district, and that had 'not been their intention when they set out from Derby.' (17) Defence, he said, asked whether they would have continued to go on begging as they left the area, having known they had committed a murder, while prosecution suggested they did not know they had killed Massey, but thought they had 'merely rendered him senseless.' (17)

Regarding the bloodstains on both men's clothing, the judge came down firmly on the side of Mr. White, County Analyst. These were early days in forensics, as has been said, but Justice Lawrence stressed the impartiality and the expertise of this witness, saying that the jury could if they liked set up their judgement against Mr. White's skill and ability, but that he 'was in the habit of seeing minute things which an ordinary person would not notice.' (17)

With regard to the prisoners resisting arrest when PC Moore came upon them at Hatton, the judge asked if this was the behaviour of men who thought that their only crime was that of begging.

Another important point, he observed, was one on which the prosecution depended, and that was the evidence of Mrs. Brassington, who saw the prisoners nearer the scene of the murder than any other person had. The prisoners denied going in the direction of Mr. Massey's farm after they had left Goldhurst Farm, but 'if Mrs. Brassington was not mistaken, they certainly did… His lordship paid considerable attention to the evidence of Mrs. Brassington and read from a transcript of the notes of the official shorthand writer.' (17)

In conclusion, Justice Lawrence said that if the jury were satisfied that 'the prisoners were guilty they should say so without the slightest hesitation, but if they had any reasonable doubt they should with equal want of hesitation acquit them.' (17) It would seem, reading from the reports in old newspapers, court records for that time not being preserved, that the judge thought the prosecution's case a strong one, that there was much circumstantial evidence against Peel and Dugan, enough to hang them. However, it was up to the jury to decide.

After two hours' deliberation, the jury returned. The verdict was 'Not Guilty.'

The prisoner's reactions were interesting and completely different. Dugan received the verdict coolly, merely staring ahead and not registering any emotion. Peel, on the other hand, was pale, and breathing hard as the verdict was given. He was described as 'deeply moved, and scarcely seemed to understand the significance of what was going on.' (19) Perhaps, like a lot more people, he could not believe his good fortune. Outside, the courtyard before County Hall was packed, and as news of the verdict reached the crowd and was passed into the nearby narrow streets and courts of the West End, where the men resided, the crowd grew even bigger, numbering in the hundreds. The wives of the prisoners were amongst the crowd and burst into tears.

Eventually, Peel and Dugan were released and, surrounded by friends and well-wishers, moved off quietly to their home at Hitchman's Lodging House.

*   *   *   *   *

The pair really do seem to have been the luckiest pair of men in Derby that day, for they had cheated the hangman, when most people seem to have thought that they would have been shortly facing the long drop at Derby Gaol. It is a tremendous responsibility to give a man the responsibility of deciding whether another person should live or die, as these jurymen were taxed with, and 'reasonable doubt' seems to have given the two beggars their freedom.

There is, in Scottish law, a third verdict that a jury can reach, apart from 'guilty' or 'not guilty'. That verdict is 'not proven', which means that sufficient evidence has not been produced to show the accused to be guilty. Reasonable doubt was established in the mind of the jury at Peel's and Dugan's trial to persuade them that it was possible that someone else could have murdered old Massey. Not proven would have probably been a fairer verdict, had it been available.

But did they actually do the murder? It seems, on the face of all the evidence, that they did. Consider their attitude when begging, that of slight menace, most beggars aiming to arouse sympathy and begging alone, aiming to arouse pity, not fear. These begged as a pair, were menacing where it suited them and were described as 'looking rough and dirty,' It seems people gave them money to go away, not because they believed their story or felt sorry for them. As to their not being near the Massey property, Mrs. Brassington saw the couple (she positively identified them in magistrates court) heading 'at a good rate' towards the cowshed. They said not, but who would you rather believe?

Consider now Mr. Massey, a man very fit and strong still. So much younger than his years that a newspaper quoted a friend 'who saw him at work in his garden last week declared that he exhibited a good deal of physical vigour, and he is confident that if attacked he would offer a resistance such as few men of his years would be capable of.' (20) He was a man, his son told the court, could be 'hasty' in his dealings with tramps. No wonder, as he had been hard-working all his life, and had had direct experience as Overseer at Burton Workhouse and administrator of the Poor Relief in his parish with poverty. He had dealt with poor and destitute people and also, no doubt, the professional beggars who just about managed to scrape a living with a hard-luck story. He would have known that the penalty for begging under the old Vagrancy Law was up to a month in prison with hard labour. Perhaps he even threatened the intruders onto his property with such a punishment. 'Hasty' was probably a generous understatement to apply to what Massey's reaction to beggars such as Peel and Dugan would have been.

One can imagine the two young men seeing Massey go to his barn as they walked back to Derby. They would have followed him across the field, desperate for some money, and, entering the cowshed, 'singing the song' as they called it to him. He probably smelled the beer they had drunk all day and berated them as work-shy spongers. Dugan, being the most truculent of the two, would have responded most aggressively. Maybe Massey raised the stool to drive them off, or they came too close and he raised it as protection, probably even threatened to have the law on them, since he would have known it so well, and the unequal fight began... A punch to the eye, one of them wrested the stool from the old man's grasp, and then, according to Peel, who said Dugan did it, the stool was brought down with great force on Massey's head, causing a compound fracture to the skull. Kicked while he was down, they attempted to rifle his pockets, but he grasped firmly on to something in his right pocket, and though they got the keys, which they discarded, and a knife, he would not let go. One of them opened the knife and slashed up and down at the pocket of the farmer's trousers with the sharp blade, cutting Massey's finger to the bone. He would have let go then. They probably ran from the barn not knowing how much they had got. Somewhere close to the house, maybe at Trusley Brook, for they went back that way, they washed the blood from their hands, Peel tore away a blood-soaked sleeve which would have incriminated him immediately if stopped, and they discarded the sleeve, the knife and the purse, keeping a mere threepence for the life they had taken. It would be interesting to know how much of a search for the discarded items the police made, for the two beggars would not have taken such incriminating evidence very far and did not have much time to hide it before they reached Goldhurst Farm, minutes after the murder, Peel looking agitated, asking for an old shirt, Dugan hanging back, not speaking.

And, if it wasn't Peel and Dugan who entered Massey's cowshed and left in a matter of minutes, leaving the old man dying, who else could it have been? The simple answer is – no one. Although only six miles from the busy town of Derby, Dalbury and its environs was a rural backwater, and few people who did not have some sort of connection or business with the place ventured down the small lanes to the villages there. As one reporter observed on the day after the murder: 'To show what a solitary and sequestered place it is, one has only to say that for two hours at a stretch all the traffic that passed consisted of two milk carts, while not a single pedestrian made his appearance.' (20) Not one person in two hours.

The people who lived in the area would still have been working when Massey was murdered. It was a farming district and all the men would be in the fields, and the women in or around the houses, as was customary in those days in rural areas. They had no time or opportunity to wander away from their work. Very few cars were on local roads in 1910, there were no buses, to bring a stranger in and then quickly away, as would be the case today, and though the locals were at work, it is worth noting that Peel and Dugan were noted wherever they went by such people as a postman, a roadman, a woman pushing a pram. None of these people, or the women on their doorsteps or in their orchard, saw anyone else. No one. Nor did Peel or Dugan speak to meeting any strangers on their wide circular tour of the area. After Massey's murder was reported, the Borough and County police searched the following day in a wide area and neither found anyone or heard of anyone in the area that day who did not have a legitimate reason to be there. Two other men were described and located and found to have not come within six miles of the village, which shows the scale and thoroughness of the search, which stretched as far as Burton-upon-Trent.

The motive for the attack is not clear. Maybe Massey was attacked for his money, or maybe he annoyed them so much, or was so robust in his dismissal of them from his property that he in some ways instigated their response. One newspaper paid tribute to Massey, saying ' (the attackers) did not count upon a vigorous resistance from a septuagenarian whom they met all alone; but – whoever they were – they found a great deal of mettle in the aged Derbyshire farmer, and gave effect to the desperate methods which find favour with their class. Had poor Mr. Massey meekly recognised the hopelessness of his position, and surrendered the money in his possession, he might have escaped bodily injury. His courage undoubtedly cost him his life.' (4)

Whatever happened that day, he died for three pennies, a random, opportunist crime, a poor price to put on a man's life.

Amos Peel surfaced again in the courts in short order. On Friday, 15th July, he was before the bench, along with Ruth, his wife, charged with using obscene language in Wright Street late on the previous night. A PC Goodwin gave samples of the conversation which the two offenders, 'who were evidently annoyed with each other, carried on at the highest pitch of their voices.' Amusingly, the constable told the bench that, 'Their expressions of the opinion each had of the other were so vile that the officer… apprehended them.' Mrs Peel nobly told the court that it was all her fault, and that her husband didn't swear at all, while Peel was equally gallant, saying that it was all through him that his wife was in her present predicament, that he had refused to go to bed until she fetched him another half pint of beer. He excused it all by saying that 'he had only recently passed through a trying ordeal and experience (possibly the first recorded instance of PTSD being used as an excuse in court!) and 'if the Bench would give him one more chance he would never trouble them again.' (21) Fined five shillings (25p), inclusive of costs.

Then in 21st August the following year, 1911, Amos was seen on Thursday evening, outside his home in Goodwin Street, making toys to sell the following day, when he suddenly put his hand to his head, and died a few minutes later. At the subsequent inquest the

John Massey's grave in All Saints' Churchyard, Dalbury Lees

doctor gave his diagnosis as death caused by a valvular disease of the heart and that verdict was returned accordingly.

John Dugan disappeared completely. Nothing more is heard of him in Derbyshire, or of his wife. Perhaps he went back to Dumfries or some other part of Scotland, for it is likely that he was of Scottish origin. Perhaps he enlisted in 1914, as many men did of his age, and died in the Great War. We will never know. He and Peel have vanished with no further trace or memorial to them.

In the churchyard of All Saints' Church, Dalbury Lees, you may still see the dark and ornate, lichen-encrusted gravestone of John Massey, with the pious assurance that 'Them also who sleep in Jesus will God bring with them.' As for his killers, if there truly is an afterlife and Day of Judgement, Peel and Dugan will not be able to count on a jury which applies 'reasonable doubt' in the final verdict.

REFERENCES

1. *The Derbyshire Advertiser & Journal*, Friday 29th April 1910.
2. *The Nottingham Journal*, Thursday 30th June 1910.
3. *The Nottingham Daily Express*, Wednesday 27th April 1910.
4. *The Derby Daily Telegraph*, Wednesday 29th June 1910.
5. *The Derby Daily Telegraph*, Wednesday 4th May 1910.
6. *The Derbyshire Advertiser & Journal*, Friday 6th May 1910.
7. *The Derbyshire Advertiser & Journal*, Friday 13th May 1910.
8. *The Derby Daily Telegraph*, Wednesday 29th April 1910.
9. *The Derbyshire Advertiser & Journal*, Saturday 2nd July 1910.
10. *The Belper News and Derbyshire Telephone*, Friday 6th May 1910.
11. *The Nottingham Evening News*, Wednesday 11th May 1910.
12. *The Nottingham Evening News*, Friday 6th May 1910.
13. *The Nottingham Evening News*, Friday 29th April 1910.
14. *The Sheffield Daily Telegraph*, Thursday 30th June 1910.
15. *The Derby Daily Telegraph*, Friday 1st July 1910.
16. *The Sheffield Evening Telegraph*, Wednesday 29th June 1910.
17. *The Derby Daily Telegraph*, Thursday 30th June 1910.
18. *The Nottingham Evening Post*, Wednesday 27th April 1910.
19. *The Illustrated Police News*, Saturday 9th July 1910.
20. *The Derby Daily Telegraph*, Tuesday 26th April 1910.
21. *The Derby Daily Telegraph*, Friday 15th July 1910.

MURDER WITH A PENKNIFE
Albert Robinson, Hadfield, Glossop,
2ND October 1880

y all accounts, Albert Robinson, who lived at Hadfield, near Glossop was a moody, taciturn young man. Although he looked a few years older, he was only twenty at the time he committed murder and was already married and the father of an eleven-week-old child and stepfather to two more children. His wife, Eliza Jane, who was ten years older than him had been married before. Eliza was described as being 'a woman of indifferent reputation.' (1) Some said that Albert had married her to spite his mother, who at the age of fifty-four, had taken a second husband herself, and one much younger too. Such a great responsibility on a young man must have contributed to the stresses in the marriage, for it was agreed by most people that it was not a happy one. They seem to have argued all the time, and to make matters worse, both of them were given to drinking heavily, and the two factors combined on the evening of Saturday, 2nd of October to bring about the untimely deaths of both of them, Eliza that very day, and Albert some months later, at the end of a rope placed there by Mr. Marwood, public hangman.

The Robinsons lived at number 62 Station Road, a corner property on one of the many terraces built for the millworkers. Albert, a stalwart young fellow, though very pale of features, which made him appear ill to some including the judge at his trial, worked as a weaver at Platt's Mills (some newspapers report he was a spinner), while his wife stayed home and minded their new child. To help their finances they had a series of lodgers, and only five days before their final row, a new one, Ellen Campbell, an

Station Road, Hadfield

unmarried woman working as a washerwoman, had taken up lodgings with them. She was to be one of the two witnesses to the murder of Eliza Robinson.

Eliza was the the daughter of a Mr. and Mrs. Clayton who had kept the Church Inn, near Newton railway station, four miles away from Hadfield, but Mr. Clayton had died in America, and Eliza's mother according to local reports, never marrying again, raised her child well on her own, moving to keep the Hirstclough toll-bar, midway between Broadbottom and Mottram. Eliza was a beautiful young woman and had a good name locally at the time, being part of the Christian Brethren, member of the Church choir, Sunday School scholar and acted in the Church Drama Society. At about twenty years of age, she met and married a young man called James Sidebottom, described as 'a steady young man of respectable connections'.(5) She bore him two children, boys named Frank, who was seven at the time of the tragedy, and Willie, who was three. But James fell ill, as did her mother, so Eliza moved into the toll-bar with James, to care for him and her mother and manage the tolls. Shortly after, both her mother and husband died and she was left alone to fend for herself and children.

Exactly what the newspapers of the day mean is not clear, but Eliza began to get a name for herself, one paper saying darkly that 'it was here that her character lowered, and here that she met Albert Robinson'. (5) Out of desperation, it seems, she allowed Robinson to talk her into marriage, for she didn't love him by her own admission, telling a friend who asked her why she had married such a known 'wild young fellow' as him:

'What was she to do as circumstances were with her? Her friends and relations had disowned her; she was left almost destitute with her two little children, and to secure a home for them she married Albert Robinson as a last resort.' (5)

Eliza tried to make a good home for Albert. She brought the few pieces of furniture she and her husband had possessed to their home in Hadfield, with tasteful (for the time) pictures on the walls, and some books of 'a decidedly moral and religious tone'. (5) At first they were managing to make the best of their 'impoverished circumstances' (5), but their finances were constrained by 'a fondness for drink' (5) and a further encroachment upon Albert's earnings in the form of a judgement against him of three shillings a week for an illegitimate child he had fathered. When Eliza became pregnant and bore Albert a son, times became really hard for them. Albert was not accustomed to having to go without; he was an only son and a spoilt one, apparently, and Eliza was known to speak her mind, so the bickering was constant. She had married for support, not to have to shoulder the responsibility of caring for a man-child like Albert, and not loving him in the first place must have made it even more intolerable.

On the last morning of her life Eliza had gone to Platt's mill at about seven in the morning with her children, and Albert had come out to her. As a paper reported, 'After some conversation and high words, (she) told him she intended to leave him.' (1) They continued to argue, but Eliza was adamant, and eventually Albert left work and came away with her. They then seem to have spent the best part of the day drinking around Hadfield, some of the time in each other's company and finishing off together in the Palatine at Hadfield.

It seems reasonably clear that the argument was about a locked box containing sixteen shillings which Eliza and her son had managed somehow to save, and which they looked upon as theirs, rightfully. Albert had seized the box that very day and had the key to it. He needed the money to pay off arrears of thirty shillings to the mother of his illegitimate child, or as he told Eliza, the mother of the girl he had seduced 'would be putting him in the crib (gaol) again.' (5) That would be why Eliza had gone so early to Albert's place of work – to attempt to get her money back, and why she said that she was going to leave him, though where she would have gone, and how she would have managed isn't said. It is small wonder the poor woman got drunk that day.

It isn't mentioned in reports from the time who was looking after the baby and the other two children, possibly Ellen Campbell, but at around four o'clock in the afternoon, Eliza came home 'a very long way on' in drink, as Ellen was to later testify. (2) Ellen and Martha Kershaw, a neighbour and friend of Eliza's, helped her upstairs to bed, and about a quarter of an hour later, Albert came home. He was upset to see the fire had been let out and rekindled it and sat by it for a while. He must have been brooding on the troubled relationship he had with Eliza, for he remarked to Campbell that it was miserable, and she replied to him that it was miserable for everybody in the house. Albert then went up and rested in another room, separate from his wife.

After about an hour or so, Eliza came down and asked Campbell when her husband had gone out and was surprised to hear that he was still upstairs. In the course of a conversation she told the washerwoman that she 'had a good mind to go upstairs and see if Albert had any money in his pocket' (3) Unfortunately, Albert was on his way downstairs and heard his wife planning to pick his pocket, and he entered the room and said, 'I suppose you thought I was asleep, but I was not asleep, if you think I am,' (3) and the bickering continued. Eliza seemed to have sobered somewhat, and Campbell testified later that she could not tell that Albert had been drinking, but both of them seem to have been out of sorts with each other. Perhaps both of them were thinking that they hadn't got out of the marriage what they had hoped for and were realising how desperate their situation was. Ruin and the workhouse beckoned, for Albert only had to fall ill, be laid off work, and Eliza to lose her pittance of money from Albert, or for the police to lock him up for failing to pay child support, and that is where they would all finish up.

Albert told Eliza to prepare tea. She prepared it, and they were all sitting down to eat it, when her neighbour and friend, Martha Kershaw, walked in. She was probably the one who sealed Eliza's fate, for as well as bringing some milk for the baby, she decided to tell Albert some home truths. She told him he ought to treat his wife better, and not quarrel with her, and then she told him that he ought to give Eliza the key to the box of money he had taken, and give her control over it. Kershaw told him that she had known his wife before she was married to him, and 'believed her to be a careful manager.' (4) Albert asked her who she was talking to, and she said, 'to you of course,' (4) and she was told to mind her own business. Martha retorted that it was her business, and that she had brought some milk for the baby , and at this Albert said he didn't send for her, and to get out of the house, and as she was leaving Kershaw warned him darkly that 'he had better mind'. (4) It was an ominous statement that probably goaded Albert further.

In a rage, Albert stood and bolted the door behind the meddling neighbour, then said to his wife, 'You've been out to fetch that person in I suppose.' Eliza denied it, saying she hadn't been out that afternoon, and Albert replied, 'Yes you have; you have been among the neighbours, telling them about me.' (4)

Eliza said to Albert, 'No I have not. You are beginning again about nothing.' (4) She stood at the front door for some time, no doubt wondering what on earth she was going to do, things had become so bad for her, and then Albert told her to get the children some tea and said to her as she came back in to the room, 'You are drunk,' and Eliza replied, 'I have had nothing but what you have paid for.' (4) and went over and stood by the baby's cradle by the fire and began rocking the child.

Albert got up from the table and went over to a drawer and reached inside. Ellen Campbell later testified that she thought she saw something in Albert's hand. Ellen Campbell got up and went and sat near Eliza, and then she heard her say to Albert, 'Don't touch me with that knife; if you do it will be the worse for you.' (2) Albert came closer and Eliza cried out, 'Save me; don't let him touch me!' and Campbell stood up and asked Albert, 'Have you got a knife?' (2) and then saw that the young man was holding a thick-bladed penknife down by his right leg. Albert went up to

Eliza and gave her a shove with both hands, then held her with his left hand and put his hand to his waistcoat pocket, where he must have stowed his knife for a moment. Eliza realised that her life was in danger, and shouted 'Murder!', and Ellen Campbell ran to the door and unbolted it. As she was leaving hurriedly, she turned and saw Albert had gripped his wife around the neck with both hands. It was enough for Ellen, and she rushed out into the yard behind the houses, shouting, 'There is a man killing his wife with a knife.' (2) By the time she returned, Eliza was lying near death on the floor, her head by the oven, with horrendous wounds to her neck

The only witness to the actual murder was Eliza's son, Frank, who later gave evidence against his stepfather. Described by various papers as a 'bright' young boy, he saw his stepfather take a penknife from his waistcoat pocket and stab his mother in the right cheek whilst holding her down and kneeling on her. He too ran out of the door shouting murder, and neighbours responded. Abraham Kershaw, husband of the woman who had given Albert a piece of her mind ran to tell a nearby Police Inspector by the name of Charlton, and as he returned he saw Albert run out into the night. It was close to quarter to nine at night.

Mrs Kershaw ran into the house and found Eliza lying, near to death, a cut running from her mouth down to her neck, blood pooling on the floor. She was placed on a sofa, and within fifteen minutes Doctor Burnett of Mottram and Doctor William Binn arrived but could do nothing for the poor woman. She had a terrible gash starting at her left ear and finishing almost beneath the chin. Her jugular vein was completely severed, and she died about three quarters of an hour later.

Meanwhile the search was on for the murderer, and it was surmised by the police that he would go to his mother's beer house, a mile away. Albert wasn't at the Bull's Head (he had taken a circuitous route to evade any pursuit, but shortly after the police left his mother was locking up for the night when there came a frantic knocking on the back door. She hurried to open it, her young husband at her side. Albert virtually fell through the door. He had made an attempt to cut his own throat and was holding a handkerchief to the wound. True to the conventions of Victorian melodrama he gasped, 'Mother, kiss me!' then collapsed, blood pouring down his chest.

One can see how the murder came about when one examines that last occurrence in the bloody murder. All his life, until a year before, Albert had been cosseted by his mother. He had grown used to the idea that women provided, and that they adored him. Described as a youth of 'weak intellect', (1) he married to spite her, as she had taken a husband close to his own age, and he had in the past few weeks found every other woman's hand against him: the grandmother and the mother of his illegitimate child who were out for his blood, wanting to put him in gaol for non-payment of maintenance; his own wife who objected to his theft of her money and was set on leaving him, the neighbour Mrs. Kershaw; even the lodger, Ellen Campbell had told him how things really stood! Unable to cope with reality, he stabbed and slashed and then ran, back to the only woman who loved him unconditionally – his mother. There he would die in her arms. She had made the monster. If any safety were to be found, it would be with her.

Dr. Burnett was sent for and found Albert lying on a sofa. His windpipe was almost completely severed but he had missed the jugular. The police followed hard on his heels and remained on guard over him. Until he recovered, he was left at the Bull's Head with a police guard.

An inquest was held on the Tuesday evening at the Palatine Inn, which was the last pub that Albert and Eliza drank in together. It was an open and shut case, and after hearing the two witnesses to Robinson's attack on his wife and the medical evidence the jury, after just a few minutes, returned a verdict of wilful murder against Albert Robinson.

Four months after the murder, on Thursday 10th February 1881, Albert Robinson was brought before the Crown Court in Derby at the Winter Assizes and indicted for the wilful murder of his wife, Jane Eliza Robinson at Glossop in the county of Derbyshire on 2nd October 1880. The Judge was Justice Denman. Mr. Horace Smith appeared for the prosecution and Mr. Etherington Smith had the thankless task of defending Robinson. By the direction of the judge a seat in the dock was provided for the prisoner. He was described as looking several years older than his stated age, 'having a large manly face, and whiskers and moustache.' (6) Throughout the trial

Robinson sat in a relaxed position, 'showing little or no concern in the proceedings.' (6) His face was described as ashen, and on several occasions Justice Denman questioned this, concerned for his health.

Albert pleaded 'not guilty' to the charge, but the only defence, given the solid eye witnesses, was going to be a plea of insanity, and this was going to be the line of defence Etherington Smith took. He was anticipated, however, by prosecuting counsel, Horace Smith, who said in his opening speech, after stating the facts of the case, that he 'couldn't conceive how there could be any doubt in the case', (6) and that:

'From what he read in the depositions (sworn statements taken from witnesses prior to the trial), he thought it just possible that the suggestion might be made that the prisoner was not in his right mind at the time when he committed the offence alleged against him. At present he could not deal with that question, but he would ask the jury to pay great attention to all the facts of the case tending to throw any light on the point whether the man, at the time, had any reasonable motive for what he did, and whether he acted as a sane man would do, although a very wicked man.' (6)

Witnesses produced by the prosecution were Ellen Campbell and Frank Sidebottom, Eliza's seven year-old son, who both testified to the actual murder, Mrs. Kershaw, who came in afterwards to find Eliza dying on the hearth, Abraham Hearnshaw, a neighbour who alerted the police and also saw Robinson flee the house, three police who testified to apprehending Robinson, and the surgeon to Derby goal. He testified, damningly for Albert, that he had seemed of sound mind, and told the doctor he was eating and sleeping well, and that he 'was perfectly composed,' (2) which must have given the jury the impression that the prisoner was a sane, cold-blooded killer.

When the defence did try to stablish insanity on Albert's part, Mr Etherington Smith was not helped by interventions from the judge, who allowed him no latitude whatsoever. Smith was cross-examining Dr. William Binns, the doctor called to both Eliza and Albert on the night of the murder of Eliza and Albert's attempted suicide, and the defence brought the subject round to Albert's father's supposed peculiarity, which the doctor said he did not know of, but admitted that an aunt of the prisoner was 'a little weak in her intellectual faculties.' (2) Smith then got the doctor to agree that 'if members of the family in one generation had to be put under restraint, it would be a strong predisposing cause to insanity,' and also to concur that often insanity was shown by a person committing suicide, as Albert had attempted. Defence seemed to be making something of a strong impact on the jury, but they took it too far for the doctor and the judge when Etherington Smith asked if the absence of motive would not strengthen the suspicion (of insanity). The doctor said flatly that he could not say, and here the judge interjected:

'His Lordship remarked that there were thousands and thousands of murders in which the motive was not proved, and in which the persons committing the murders were not insane.' (2)

Bravely, Etherington Smith plugged on. He asked the doctor about the term 'irresistible impulse,' but again the judge struck it out, saying 'Such a thing as "irresistible impulse" was bad law and bad everything.' (2) Changing tack slightly the defence counsel desperately asked the doctor if it was not evidence of insanity for a person to attack a near relative, and the judge seems to have lost patience here, for he said, the 'question was absurd when one came to consider the number of murders committed on relatives.' (2) The doctor, too, slapped the idea down comprehensively, saying that it was more likely for a near relative to be attacked 'as there were greater chances of provocation.' He did admit, however, that 'a silent and somewhat melancholy temperament was akin to derangement of the mind.' (2) This was obviously a reference to earlier testimony by Ellen Campbell that Albert had been very moody and withdrawn the whole week she had stayed there, and barely spoke.

In his case for the defence, Etherington Smith tried to convince them that there was insanity in the family and that Robinson was not in control of himself when he attacked his wife and killed her. He admitted it was difficult to prove and said 'The defence were labouring under some difficulties.' (2) He said that they hadn't been '…able to bring witnesses from all parts of the county, and trace all the history of the family.' (2) He asked the jury to bear that in mind, which, really was tantamount to saying he couldn't prove it but they should believe him. He said that one thing was not in doubt: 'the prisoner was silent, moody, and of a somewhat melancholy habit and manner.' (2) He pointed out that in the last few days Robinson had barely spoken, and claimed that a madness had overtaken him. He further tried to say there was no motive for the murder, and this proved the madness, and talked of a 'taint' in the family that had overtaken Albert Robinson too, against which he had been powerless, saying, "…"the overmastering influence" of this taint had led him to commit such a deed.' (2) Proof of this sudden bout of insanity was also shown when he had tried to commit suicide after the horrific murder. The only defence witness that was put up in the witness box was William Middleton, Albert's young stepfather, who claimed that the prisoner's uncle was 'an eccentric man – not sharp,' and that 'prisoner was wild before he was married, but had conducted himself well since,' and 'was a good workman.' (2) As the only defence witness, that was indeed pathetic.

The prosecution counsel dismissed any defence of insanity effectively with a short speech to the jury in which he demolished every point the very weak defence had proposed. He said:

'It was perfectly clear the prisoner had a motive in doing what he did. There could be no doubt that he was considerably irritated at the conduct of his wife in her getting drunk and telling tales to the neighbours. His sullenness was an evidence of his discontent, not of insanity. If there was insanity in the prisoner's family why had not someone, a medical man if possible, been called to prove it? The prisoner's attempt to take his own life did not show his insanity; it was quite reasonable, when the man had murdered his wife, that he should desire to take the next step, and that he should desire to cut his own throat.' (6)

It was left to His Lordship, Lord Denman, to sum up, and he did so at length. He looked every inch a High Court Judge in his scarlet robes, a handsome, aged man, indeed a contemporary said of Justice Denman in a somewhat barbed article titled, 'An Ornament on the Bench,' that he looked a model judge but was never quite so good a judge as he looked.'! (7) Denman explained the law regarding a person taking away another's life and said that no one was justified in yielding to impulse and should restrain themselves.

In a case of wilful murder, he said that it was the job of the prisoner's counsel to prove that 'at the time the deed was done, he did not know the difference between right and wrong.' (6) It seems clear, looking at the absence of any really strong witnesses to make this point for defence, that Etherington Smith had failed there. As to his argument that Robinson's attempt at suicide was evidence of his insanity, '… his lordship said that sometimes heartless, cruel brutes, who had robbed others, and used violence, when the time came for them to take their trial attempted to take away their lives.' (6)

This must have registered with the jury, particularly the judge using emotive terms such as 'heartless' and 'cruel' for if any crime fitted those epithets, then this was surely the one. Within two minutes (some papers put it at one minute), the jury found Robinson guilty, and did not add a recommendation for mercy, as they were entitled to, and which some observers had expected, given Robinson's age. The sheer brutality of this murder had out-weighed any sympathy anyone could have had for his youth.

The prisoner, who had stood for the verdict, was asked by the Clerk of Arraigns if he had anything to say, but remained mute. The customary black cap was then placed on Justice Denman's head and he delivered the following address:

'Albert Robinson, you have been found guilty of this crime of wilful murder, and the facts were too plain for any jury or judge to entertain a shadow of a doubt that on the 2nd of October you killed and murdered your wife. God only knows what might have been the whole motive for that act; you yourself know, but no other human being. I don't wish to speculate further upon them. You might have had some things which to a certain extent aroused you to anger and disturbed the free balance of your mind. But you have committed this terrible crime; you have committed it upon the person of your wife, and I cannot hold out any hope at all to you that the sentence which I am about to pass will not be carried out, and that before very few days are over you will have to pay the penalty of this your act upon the scaffold. I therefore can only implore, and I do so most earnestly, to employ the few days remaining to you upon earth in making your peace with that God whom you have offended.

'It is the sentence of this court that you be taken from hence to the place from whence you came, and from thence to a place of execution, and that you there be hanged by your neck until you are dead, and that your body be buried within the precincts of the gaol, and may the Lord have mercy upon your soul.' (6)

It is recorded that Robinson was 'remarkably passive and stolid,' and turned round and left the dock rail in an apparently unconcerned manner.'(2)

In the short time left, there were two attempts made to gain a reprieve for Robinson by setting up public appeals, known as 'memorials' to the Home Secretary. Lord Howard of Glossop, the Liberal politician, communicated with the vicar of Hadfield, also named Hadfield, to convene a public meeting, and fifty or so people attended. So strong was the feeling against Robinson that but for the casting vote of the vicar as chairman, it would not have been passed. In Derby a petition was taken round, but received little support, most people seeming to feel that the law should take its course and Robinson deserved his punishment. Neither petition gained any sympathy from the Home Office.

One of the least concerned about the whole procedure seems to have been Robinson himself. As one reporter said, 'he maintained the utmost indifference to the fate which awaited him from the time of his arrest until the latest hour of his life.' (8) He settled in to await the hangman, asking for tobacco and beer, slept well throughout, and ate with a good appetite. His mother and other relatives made the long trip from Hadfield and visited him in Vernon Street Gaol on the last Wednesday, and friends and acquaintances on the Friday and Saturday, and he was very calm and composed while making his farewells.

The most important arrival at Derby Gaol on the Saturday, however, was Marwood the executioner, who stepped through the wicket gate at around 2 pm that afternoon, with little fuss, where he would lodge until the execution on Monday was carried through. This was a man who took his calling seriously and did a very professional job of despatching the condemned men (and women) that he was tasked with executing. Marwood prided himself on the most humane hanging he could perform, and introduced the 'Long Drop' method into England from Ireland, using a 'length of drop' table of between six and ten feet, based on the weight of the condemned person, which was designed, when placing the knot under the left ear, to break the neck rather than leave the unfortunate victim to asphyxiate. Further, he introduced the split trapdoor and did away where possible with the steps up to the scaffold, so that the condemned person walked straight onto the trap instead of having to be assisted up steps, hands pinioned behind, often a difficult procedure, though there were still steps up to the scaffold at Derby Gaol at this time.

There was a famous rhyme or riddle at the time that is grimly ironic when one considers Albert Robinson's situation as he sat in the condemned cell at Derby. It ran, 'If Pa killed Ma, who'd kill Pa? Marwood!' and here 'Pa' Robinson was, having killed the mother of three, Eliza, waiting in the condemned cell to be killed by William Marwood, who was on record as saying that he considered what he was preparing to do as being God's work.

However, it didn't seem to worry Robinson in the slightest that he was facing death in a few days, a newspaper reporting that 'a quiet demeanour has characterised him all along.' (9), and another saying, 'he manifested the utmost indifference as to his condition.' (5). He was counselled frequently by the prison chaplain, the Reverend H. Moore, and 'listened with great attention.' (9) On Sunday, his last full day on earth, he attended Divine Service twice, and 'seemed very earnest in his expressions of regret.' (9)

It was a cold, clear day on Monday 28th February 1881 when Robinson went to the scaffold. The air was sharp with frost and snow lay on the ground. Despite the bitter coldness of the weather, shortly after seven in the morning over 200 people had gathered outside the gaol to see the black flag, hoisted when the execution had taken place, rise up above the Vernon Street Gaol walls. The crowd was mostly, one paper primly reported, people '…belonging almost entirely to the artisan class. Persons of a better class were scarcely to be found.' (E) *The Derbyshire Advertiser* further recorded that 'Inspector Adams and a number of police officers were stationed in the vicinity, but their presence was not needed, as the crowd were very orderly in their behaviour, and no unseemly remarks were made except by a few youths.' (10)

Inside the gaol, Marwood had been making all ready on the

scaffold, and at a quarter to eight he walked to the pinioning room where Albert had been brought from the condemned cell by the warders, the under-sheriff, a sheriff's officer, and the prison chaplain. There, the prisoner's hands were pinioned behind him by Marwood, with leather restraints the executioner had made himself, being a shoemaker by trade, and the procession was led out to the scaffold, with the chaplain praying aloud as they walked. At the foot of the scaffold, the procession stopped while Robinson repeated a prayer. He seemed quite prepared to meet his fate, and said to the assembled officials, 'I hope God will pardon my sin, and I think he will. I do not fear this scaffold.' (9) He then ascended the steps without assistance, managing even the top step, which was a high one. He took his place under the beam of the scaffold with very little direction, and the rest is best described to the one reporter who was allowed in as a witness:

'(Robinson)… moved his feet in a careful manner when Marwood sought to place him with exactness. He still continued to say, "O, Lord, receive my spirit," The executioner then took from his pocket the white cap, and drew it down over the face of the condemned man, and at the same time adjusted the rope, which he had previously thrown over his head. He (Marwood) spoke to him in an assuring tone, and then, having left the scaffold, instantly drew the bolt. The platform gave way with less than its usual noise. The drop was about eight feet… sufficient to break the vertebrae. One slight shudder seemed to pervade the body, and then one revolution of the rope, and all was still.' (9)

Outside the massive gates of the prison, the crowd, described as 'consisting largely of roughs' (11) by one paper, had by now swelled to around 500 strong, and as the clock inside the gaol had begun to ring the fatal hour, a deep silence fell over the assemblage. As the last chime sounded the bolt of the trapdoor was clearly heard being drawn, and a collective murmur came from the people outside.

'Almost at the same time, the black flag was drawn up the staff over the entrance to the gaol and floated in the bright morning air.' (11) Albert Robinson had paid the ultimate price for his savage murder.

There is an intriguing footnote to the Hadfield murder, however, for some thirty years before Albert Robinson killed his wife so savagely there had been an equally bloody murder in the area. This one, however, was never solved, until – maybe – the Robinson case was being discussed in the papers.

On Thursday 16th January, 1851, an old lady called Mary Kinder, who lived at the isolated Higher Cliff Farm at Werneth Low, near Hattersley, and five miles from Hadfield, was battered to death in her parlour, between five and six o'clock in the evening. Her head was split open with a heavy, blunt instrument, such as a mallet, which was never found, nor was any suspect ever detained. There were no witnesses to the savage murder, the servants out at milking in the shippons, and her two unmarried daughters visiting friends a few miles away. Robbery had been the motive, it seems, for drawers had been rifled, and some money was missing, but a larger amount had been overlooked, as if the murderer had been disturbed in his search or had been aware of having to be hasty. A reward of £300 pounds was offered for information and a free pardon to any accomplice not actually involved in the murder who would give up the guilty person. No one ever came forward, and the murder went unsolved and unpunished.

Thirty years later, in early December of 1880, with Robinson languishing in Derby Gaol awaiting trial, an intriguing piece appeared, first in local papers, then republished in many other national and other newspapers. It recounted the tale of the old murder, then added the startling information that:

'A letter has been received from America this week which seems to throw some light on the mystery. A former resident in the district where the murder was committed had been furnished by a friend in this country with a copy of a paper containing a report of the Hadfield murder (committed a few weeks since), and in acknowledging the gift he refers to the crime which has so long been a mystery, and says that a man named Clayton, who lately died in America, confessed before his death that he murdered Mrs. Kinder. Clayton is still remembered by old residents in the district.' (12)

Robinson's wife, remember, was a Clayton before marriage to her first husband; her father, a local man, was a publican who went to America, where it was said he died, leaving his wife and child to find their own way in the world. If Eliza's mother never remarried, was it because her husband had not yet died, but was in America, on the run from justice in England? Was he the murderer who confessed on his deathbed? It seems very likely that it was the same man, or why would the correspondent mention it in conjunction with the later murder? We shall never know; too much time has passed, but it is a terrible, gruesome irony that possibly Eliza had both a father and a husband who committed bloody murders.

REFERENCES

1. *The Derbyshire Courier*, Saturday 9th October 1880.
2. *The Derby Mercury*, Wednesday 16th February 1881.
3. *The Derbyshire Times & Chesterfield Herald*, Saturday, 9th October 1880.
4. *The Derbyshire Advertiser & Journal*, Wednesday 11th February 1881.
5. *The Derby Daily Telegraph & Reporter*, Saturday 28th February 1881.
6. *The Nottinghamshire Guardian*, Friday 18th February 1881.
7. *Vanity Fair*, Friday 19th November 1892.
8. *The Sheffield Daily Telegraph*, Tuesday 1st March 1881.
9. *The Derbyshire Times & Chesterfield Herald*, Friday 4th March 1881.
10. *The Derbyshire Advertiser & Journal*, Friday 4th March 1881.
11. *The Derby Mercury*, Wednesday 2nd March 1881.
12. *The Manchester Evening News*, Saturday 4th December 1880.

THE HANDLEY MURDER
ELIZABETH HUDSON, HANDLEY, DERBYSHIRE
24TH APRIL 1873

Sentencing the man before him in the dock to death by hanging on July 15th, 1873, in the Crown Assizes at Derby, the judge, Mr. Justice Honyman, broke down as he pronounced the sentence. After assuming the traditional black cap, a square cloth placed over his wig, the judge spoke in a tremulous voice, and overcome with emotion he frequently sobbed as he addressed the prisoner in the dock before him.

He would have done better to have saved his tears for the condemned man's dead wife, for if ever a man deserved to hang it

The Devonshire Arms, Middle Handley.
Lisa's body was carried here and laid on a table

© 2020 Andrew Hill

139

was Benjamin Hudson. During their married life he had misused his wife Elizabeth badly, often beating her, and, finally, when she thought she had broken free of her brute of a husband, he stalked her down and savagely killed her. Quite what provoked the judge's sympathy is hard to understand when one looks at the case of the Handley Murder, as the press of the time dubbed it, but there could be an explanation, which we shall look at later.

The township of Handley, which lies in North East Derbyshire, is made up of three hamlets: Middle Handley, West Handley, and Nether Handley It is situated on high ground about two and a half miles north west of Staveley, near Chesterfield, and to the south of Sheffield, with beautiful views across the Moss Valley. The small villages of Lightwood and Marsh Lane are also close by, the latter two virtually one village. Handley was described by the Sheffield poet John Holland as being:

> "…where mingling thatch and tile
> Show'd the snug dwellings of the cottagers
> Of these who till'd their own well-cultured farms'
> "…the stately hedgerow,
> Where dog-rose, hawthorn, sloe or crab-tree blooms,
> For here tall hedgerows still divide the fields." (1)

The only industry apart from labour-intensive agriculture in the immediate area in the eighteenth and early nineteenth century had been scythe and sickle-making, soon to die with the approach of mechanised harvesting, and the rustic charm of the place was encroached upon with the coming of the railways, to service the iron ore and coal mining on the edges of the area, all of which brought more people into the area to work. The Industrial Revolution had swept into the area, and was booming, causing great social and environmental changes. One newspaper reporter bewailed its effect on the Handley district in a newspaper reporting the Handley Murder, saying that 'Handley is one of those villages beloved of painters, where nymphs and shepherds dance to the sound of the pipe, where… the ploughman treads his weary way towards home, and the milkmaid bears her pails to the dairy… in the land of beauty, harmony and peace. Such may be the ideal picture of village life.' (2) It was indeed an ideal picture, one painted by someone who had never had to labour hard and long in the fields, to endure the elements for low pay and poor treatment by the employer, or to withstand slumps in trade that meant layoffs and near-starvation. Little surprise that many farm labourers went to work in the coalmines that were opening around the township, offering less hours and higher pay, though the work was hard and there was a frequent risk of injury or death below ground. The coal mines shaped a breed of folk in Handley who had become a little different to the sniffy reporter's picturesque countryfolk:

'Instead of shepherds and shepherdesses we find foul-mouthed colliers, and village belles who give birth to illegitimate children. Oaths and threats are more freely uttered than dulcet songs, or the music of pan-pipes, and the whole population seems steeped to the lips in barbarism and ignorance.' (2)

If the reporter had cared to consider the people he so roundly condemned, whilst bemoaning the loss of some Greek fantasy of panpipes and shepherdesses that had never been, he would have seen that the majority of 'barbarians' he condemned, and who were witnesses and players in the Handley Murder were local folk trying to adapt to their circumstances in an industrial boom whilst earning a harsh, uncertain living, and far from being brute beasts who were 'steeped to the lips in barbarism', (2) Ben Hudson's actions were roundly condemned. Indeed, there was a genuine fear that the miners might lynch the man at one stage.

Consider a coalminer's life in the 1800's. Unlike the ploughman who wearily plodded home at the end of his day, and took it as a given that he would do the same on the morrow, no miner stepped out of his door at the start of his shift secure in the knowledge that he would return later. In nineteenth-century Britain more than one thousand miners were killed every year in accidents below ground. It was a risky job in mid-Victorian England, the 'getting of coal'. Miners risked rock falls, explosions or asphyxiation from poisonous gases, flooding, and all the time breathing in coal dust that gave them black lung disease or pneumoconiosis the respiratory disease. It was a harsh, hard life, and formed a man's character and his community.

* * * * *

In the old debate between nature and nurture, it would be hard to point a finger either way, though, when considering what made Ben Hudson the way he was. Although his environment had an effect upon him, from an early age he was known as a quiet, brooding person with a jealous nature. He also showed a propensity for cruelty towards small creatures, often a sign of a murderer in the making, and even his own mother said he enjoyed nothing more in life than killing, mainly rabbits. He took up poaching, as did many men in the area, who made a good secondary income in selling rabbits around the area. By the age of thirteen or fourteen he 'manifested a desire to become independent of parental control…' (3) He showed signs of wanting to be his own master, and left his parent's home at Newbold to live at a house now known as South View in West Handley, with his grandfather, Richard Hudson, whose second name he took, his father's surname being Vickers. What schooling that was offered he refused, only attending Sunday School on occasion, and he couldn't read or write as a result. By the age of thirteen or fourteen he went to work at a local coalmine, though he was not keen on regular work, preferring to spend his time in the fields, catching rabbits illegally or attending rabbit-coursing events. Eventually, Benjamin was caught poaching and only an uncle paying his fine saved him from a month in gaol. There was an earlier incident too, where Benjamin used threatening language to one James Drury, and was bound over to keep the peace. He doesn't seem to have been a heavy drinker, though he did frequent the Devonshire Arms nearby in Middle Handley, or the beer houses in the area, including one kept by another Richard Hudson, cousin to Benjamin, but many colliers visited pubs. Houses were small, and families large. The pub was their equivalent of the gentlemen's club, and in mining villages the pubs and alehouses were very much a male preserve. If women went to the pub at all, they took a drink in the kitchen with the publican's wife.

From an early age, Ben was very possessive of his cousin Eliza, one year younger than him, and it was said later that 'From a child he began to form a strong attachment to the deceased, and for years before they were married he was accustomed to work himself into a state of almost frenzied jealousy on her account, following her from place to place, and becoming greatly excited when he observed her speak in a friendly way to young men of his own age.' (3) Really, the writing was on the wall from the very beginning.

Eliza Hudson (the 'village belle' who gave birth to illegitimate children, as referred to by the *Sheffield Independent* reporter) was the oldest girl in a family of eight and would most probably have had to help at home with the younger children rather than go to school, which was not then compulsory. Like Benjamin she could not read or write, signing against her name on documents with a cross. At around fourteen years old, the age a working-class girl would be sent into domestic service away from home, and with the two sisters nearest to her age old enough to help at home, Eliza went to work at Gill's Farm, where an uncle by marriage also lived and worked, a man roughly twelve years older than Eliza. This was William Holmes, sometimes known as 'Gill', and when she was sixteen, Eliza fell pregnant by him. Illegitimacy was not uncommon at that time among the labouring classes, particularly of the first-born, but marriage was out of the question here. Eliza came home and gave birth to her first child, Mary, who was also known, as was the fashion then, as 'Polly'. This must have rankled terribly with the possessive Benjamin, and it is said that he began to abuse Eliza physically from the outset of their relationship, which began once she returned to her parent's home. A year later, Eliza became pregnant again, this time to Ben, and this does not seem to have sat well with her father, Richard Hudson, who threw her out of the house, and she had to go and live with her grandmother at Apperknowle, just over a mile away. Eliza did not marry Benjamin, probably because parental permission was required until both parties reached twenty-one years of age at that time. Possibly Eliza's parents opposed it because Benjamin was known to be of an idle disposition, and rarely in work. In those times, before social security, a man had to provide for his family or they went into the workhouse, a grim prospect indeed, and Eliza was to experience it quite soon in her life. Whatever happened, Eliza gave birth to another illegitimate child, George Hudson.

An ironstone miner called 'Staunch' or James, Hibbert soon came on the scene. He seems to have made Eliza some sort of offer, and she went to live with him in late 1869, taking her two children by two fathers with her. 'Staunch' was considerably older than Eliza, being thirty-four to her nineteen, but he seemed a decent man, which may be reflected in his nickname of 'Staunch', meaning loyal or reliable, or could have referred to his size and strength. Yet again Eliza fell pregnant, and one would have expected by the law of averages that this time Eliza might have married the baby's father. It would have seemed that marriage had been mentioned between her and 'Staunch' Hibbert, but there was a chilling threat made when 'Benjamin Hudson went to her, and said that if she did not marry him (Hudson) she should not marry anyone else. She consented, and they were married about six weeks before the child was born.' (4)

Was it just fear of him that made Eliza marry Benjamin Hudson in November or December of 1870, or did she genuinely love him? Whatever, it was a bad decision, for the ill-treatment at Ben's hands started almost immediately. Ben and Eliza were allowed to live with her parents until the baby was born, but it must have been an uncomfortable stay, for neither parent liked Ben, and the house was crowded, with six siblings of Eliza also living there and two grandparents, and shortly after Hibbert's child, a son named Alexander, was born to Eliza, there was a disagreement which could have involved the mother, for Benjamin later spoke very badly of her, and they were asked to leave.

Someone offered Eliza and Ben a house at Lightwood, just between the villages of Marsh Lane and Middle Handley, and the unhappy couple moved in there. They were no happier together, for it rankled with Ben Hudson that he was raising another man's child. He continually abused Eliza over it, and a surprising transaction eventually took place: 'The third child was so incessantly ill-treated by her husband, that she gave it away when it was eight months old to a man named Thompson and his wife.' (4) Thompson died soon after, and baby Alexander was given away again, this time to its uncle, Staunch Hibbert's brother. One hopes Alexander had a good life.

Around the time of the move to Lightwood, Ben deserted his

family, and Eliza had to endure the humiliation of going into the workhouse, but spent only one night there. Ben was in imminent danger of being hauled before court, for it was a criminal offence not to support one's wife and children then, and he could have been punished with a week in gaol. He fetched his family out just in time to prevent this but continued in his dissolute habits of poaching and rabbit coursing, avoiding work wherever possible. Eliza was often forced to go out charring at other people's houses or washing and mangling clothes to earn enough for her and the children to survive on. After a year or so, they moved back to West Handley, probably because of financial difficulties which seemed to beset them as a result of Ben's lazy ways, and which caused the frequent rows he and Eliza had.

The abuse and beatings continued, and on April 3rd, 1871, five months after their wedding, Benjamin was bound over to keep the peace by magistrates at Eckington. It had little effect on his behaviour, however. He doesn't seem, from the limited descriptions of him to have been a man whom one could reason with, or who accepted another point of view, being described later as having 'a dogged sullenness, which nothing appears to penetrate.' (5) The legal restraint was useless, and the attacks grew worse, fuelled by Hudson's resentment. In the spring of 1872, Eliza had a fourth child, but it only lived a month or so. In April of 1872, Ben beat Eliza until she was 'black and blue', then on the 25th May he beat her so badly that he was taken before the magistrates and sentenced to two months' imprisonment with hard labour at Derby Gaol on Vernon Street, and further bound over at the expiration of the sentence to be of good behaviour for six months. Under the heading of 'A Brute of a Husband,' the paper reported that 'the Bench stigmatised the offence as atrocious, and regretted that they could not award the only fitting punishment, viz., flogging (judicial corporal punishment having been taken away from local courts in the previous decade), '...for he heartily deserved it.' (6) Eliza told the court that Hudson hadn't worked for several weeks, Ben's only defence for beating her so savagely was that 'she dared him to do it.' (6)

*   *   *   *   *

The sentence must have come hard for one so used to a feckless life as Ben. Derby's new Gaol was a great improvement on the previous one, but even so life was hard. Ben had to rise at six in the morning, dress in his prison uniform, covered in the broad arrows seen in old illustrations, make up his bed in a regulated way, scrub the floor of his cell, then after breakfast, chapel service, followed by three hours of hard labour, which he must have detested. After a break for dinner, another three hours of hard labour, and in the evening, confined to his cell, picking oakum, which involved separating pieces of old rope by hand into fibres, for use in shipyards and building construction, painful to the convicts' hands, often causing them to bleed. At eight o'clock, it was lights out, no moonlit poaching forays in the fields around Handley. Far from teaching Ben a lesson, it seemed to embitter him even more.

When Hudson was sent to gaol, he gave his house up and Eliza was forced to find somewhere else for her and the children. She moved to Lightwood, close by, and washed and mangled to support her family. Hudson eventually got out, under a six-month bond to behave toward his wife, but in October of 1872 Eliza managed to break free from the little community in which she must have felt trapped in a cycle of violence. She gained a position as a domestic servant at Sheffield. One would have thought that Ben would have seen that as a solution to their unhappy relationship. Eliza would be away from the village and gossiping tongues that hurt his pride, apparently, and he could get on with his life. However, he would still have had to provide for the children, or risk going to goal. Whatever the motivation, Benjamin went to Sheffield and persuaded Eliza to come back, promising to change his ways. He didn't improve, however, and probably had no intention of doing so. He bided his time, and when his bond had elapsed, he beat Eliza severely, so badly that her own father testified that 'her head was like a mummy,' (7) and they thought her jaw was broken. What is amazing, reading now, is that no one intervened in an effectual manner, not even her own father. He said later, after his daughter was dead, that 'I have seen him (Hudson) knock her down and have seen him hit her many a time.' (7) What kind of man was it that could see his own child so abused? Richard Hudson was to be criticised for this later, and rightly so, but it was too late for poor Eliza.

A common belief in those days was that a man was allowed by law to use light punishment on his wife. It is thought that a seventeenth-century judge Francis Buller had ruled that a man may beat his wife with a stick no thicker than his thumb, giving rise to the phrase 'rule of thumb', meaning a rough and ready guide, but in fact there is no record of Buller ever making this statement. Whatever, many people were reluctant to come between a man and his wife, which is likely how Ben managed to get away with such violence towards Eliza.

Even after this beating, Eliza took Benjamin back and continued to live with him. On February 15th, 1873, he followed her into the house of Mrs Palmer, a neighbour, and 'punched and throttled her again.' (7) The violent attacks were increasing in frequency. Two months later there was a particularly nasty attack.

Martha Hardwick and her husband lived twenty yards away in a neighbouring house, and owned the house that Eliza and Ben lived in. She was 49 years old and had known Eliza since she was a child, she later testified. She was used to Eliza taking refuge at her house from Ben's rages, and on April 11th, which was Good Friday, at around quarter past five in the evening, Eliza 'ran into the house (Martha Hardwick's), with her bosom bare, and said her husband had been trying to take some cough lozenges which she had in her clothing. Her breast was red, and she looked as if she had been throttled. She was afraid to go home and stayed all night.' (8)

Martha's husband was an underviewer at the local colliery, a responsible job with some status. At 49 years old, Martha was a lot older than Ben and Eliza, and she does not sound as if she was afraid to face down Ben Hudson. She put her friend up for the night, but eventually Eliza went back to her house and her children on the Sunday.

Ben, however, was still simmering, and when he returned home he locked the door to keep her in and said to her, 'Thar just the ...... I wanted, I shall cook thy goose for thee.' (8) Eliza managed to escape again, and spent the night away, probably with Martha once more, and Eliza's father was sent for. She told him, 'Ben swears he'll murder me.' (7) It was only ten days before he acted on the threat.

When Eliza's father fetched her back to his house. Ben was skulking in the lane, 'same as if he was waiting of her,' (7) as her father later told the court. He further testified that he remonstrated with Benjamin, telling the jury: 'I said, "Ben, it's a strange queer thing thou can't live peaceable and quiet." He said nothing at first, and I said, "If thou doesn't thou'll have to be made." He said I might go to h… and made use of other foul expressions.' (7) (At Ben's trial, the insult was given as 'You can go to ….. and …. yourself.'(9))

Eliza was determined to make a final break this time, and to lay charges against Ben, too, and this would almost certainly mean another spell in prison for him. By the following Saturday he seems to have been sweating over this eventuality, because he sent friends to Richard Hudson's house, and in his testimony Richard Hudson gives a flavour of the way the locals spoke in those days:

'On the Saturday night his friends came to me, begging of my daughter not to prosecute him, as he knew if she did he would have "up t'rails to go." (i.e. arrested and taken by the railway to Derby Gaol). I told them if they talked from June to January I would not interfere.' (7) They pressed him further, but Richard said he 'was sick and tired of this work.' (8)

Chillingly, 'Hudson said to the other two men, "Never mind, I'll do the b…" ' (7)

Eliza was determined that the marriage was at an end, and when she took Ben to court this time, at Eckington magistrates, his lawyer produced some sort of agreement which 'compromised the case'. (7) This was a legal device to try and reach some understanding between the two parties. Ben had to pay his wife five shillings (25p) a week maintenance and was bound over not to injure or molest her in any way. Both parties signed their name to the agreement with a cross. Ben undertaking these conditions postponed the summons for a month. Presumably, it was a form of probation for Ben, to keep him out of goal, providing for his family, and staying away from Eliza. Eliza testified at the court that Ben was not working to support her, which, along with violence in the marriage, was one of the two legal grounds for a separation.

The agreement – Eliza no longer being under his control – clearly upset Ben, for he began to stalk her. He had nothing else to do, being averse to work and unable to keep a job. His last job he had been fired from, at Bainbridge and Company's Coalmine, Unstone, for turning up to work only nine days in five weeks, and he seemed to have scratched a small living by occasional odd jobs such as gardening around Handley. He also sold everything in the house that Eliza had fled from. Now, if he needed to stay out of gaol, he had to work and earn money, and if he did earn any, he didn't get to keep it. Responsibility and control were being forced on him, and he did not like it. Instead of shouldering the blame, he saw not himself as being responsible for all his troubles, but his wife; Eliza was the offender.

That he was nursing his resentment, adding to the smouldering hatred until it burst into flame is shown by one witness at his trial, Eliza's own brother, also known as Richard Hudson. He was a coal miner and also ran his own house as a beer house. Incredibly, after the beatings given to his sister by Ben Hudson, Richard still allowed him to drink there, and on Easter Monday, April 14th, Ben Hudson was in Richard's beer house, drinking with a group of miners. Richard heard Ben Hudson talking to the group about the separation from his wife, and Hudson said that a miner called John Crofts told Ben that he would 'be living with her again before the week's out.' (7) Ben said, '"I'll bet a gallon of beer I don't live with her in a month, and I'll bet another gallon I do something to be talked about." ' (7) Richard Hudson said that Ben didn't expand on what that 'something' would be, but that Benjamin was sober at the time.

* * * * *

His resentment towards Eliza simmered in Ben's twisted mind for the rest of that week, and as Eliza showed every intention of not communicating in any way, it grew. On the night before Eliza's death, a friend of Ben's called John Morton came home in the afternoon of Wednesday the 23rd April and found Ben in his house (Ben was homeless at this stage and relying on the goodness of friends for food and shelter). John lived at Lightwood, close to Ben's last house, so it's possible that he was spying on Eliza too, seeing if she was revisiting the area. For some twisted reason, although he hated her, he wanted her back. And if she wouldn't come back…

Morton didn't say what Ben wanted at his house, but it is highly likely that they went poaching rabbits together, for they walked towards Handley together, and at the end of this fairly purposeless walk, coming back about nine o'clock at night, Morton testified that Hudson gave him two nets and three wires used for catching rabbits, and a broken whistle, saying 'he should very likely not want them any more.' (7) Ben knew that Morton had a gun, and 'he said if I would lend him this gun he "Would shoot both his wife and the old b…" I think he meant his wife's mother by this expression.' (7) We don't know much of Eliza's mother; she does not appear at the inquest or the trial. She was a busy woman, with a large family of her own, ten children in all surviving, but she went to court with Eliza to gain an order against Ben, and seems to have been more proactive against Ben than any of the local men, and that is probably why he bore such a grudge towards her. Ben seems to have talked about nothing but 'getting even' with Eliza for what he saw as his unreasonable treatment. He told Morton while they were out in the fields that Eliza was 'thick with other men,' (7) and said that James Hibbert, whom she had lived with, and whom Ben had taken her away from and married, had been talking about Eliza, and had 'said that he would give him (Hudson) a sovereign (£1.00) for her if he would let him take her back. He then said neither Hibberd nor no one else should have her, for he would be her end.' (7) Chillingly, they talked of this as they passed the place where Eliza would meet her end in a few days. Morton tried to talk Ben out of his crazy plans. He told Ben, 'For God's sake, never do anything of the kind. If thou can get this week over, thou shall go right away and work with me.' (7)

Ben's problem was that he had to somehow find five shillings (25 pence) to pay the police at Eckington for the maintenance of Eliza's two children, and he had to find it every week, or he would go to gaol. He told Morton that he had no work, except for a day or two at Richard Hudson's, gardening. The pressure was increasing. On Wednesday he visited a former neighbour at Lightwood who was a friend of Eliza's and told her to ask Eliza for two bills he had to pay. The woman, Emily Cobb, asked Eliza, but she refused to hand them over, probably knowing that Ben could not pay and would destroy them. She told Emily to ask Ben for the money instead. Eliza was in the area, spending the night away from her parents' house, doing some cleaning for an old friend and neighbour, Martha Hardwick and staying the night at her house, not returning to Handley.

Ben stayed at an uncle's house for some of the time, but for the rest he was, as one correspondent termed it, 'living a vagrant life'. (10) and hanging around the area, visiting houses Eliza visited and trying to affect a meeting. He seems to be hoping to chance upon Eliza, maybe negotiate some sort of reconciliation. He could not live with her, but he couldn't manage without her. For her part, Eliza was trying to evade him. It was a deadly game of cat and mouse which would end badly for both.

If Ben's intentions weren't plain he made them so when he later visited Jane Evan's house. Ben's poaching friend, Morton, lodged with the Evan's family, but he wasn't in on this occasion. Jane tackled him about his recent maintenance order and asked Hudson how he was going to manage to pay the five shillings a week the court had ordered him to pay to Eliza. Ben gloomily told Jane that he had no work, and that 'if he could get none, he must knock some b— down.' (7) Again, he referred to the offer of a sovereign by Hibberd if he would sell his wife, and said bitterly that the man could have Eliza for five shillings. He said Hibberd and Butler, a former neighbour of whom Ben was jealous, were both in the running for her. Evans tried to reason with Ben and said that he would be better finding work and reconciling with Eliza, changing his ways and going to live with her in harmony. His chilling answer to Jane Evans was given at the adjourned inquest:

' "He said, 'Nay, the first time I light upon the b— I shall knock her b— skull in." ' (7)

Given that sworn testimony, the defence's claim at the later trial that Ben had acted on impulse cut little ice with the judge and jury. Jane was also to testify that she had heard Ben threaten his wife's life quite often, and had also seen Ben strike his wife many times and that he had even hit her, Jane Evans, when she had got between them to protect Eliza. She told the jury that she 'had been struck by chairs, and once by a coal rake (a fire iron) when I have attempted to part them.' (4)

∗   ∗   ∗   ∗   ∗

Eliza did not go back to her parents and her children that night. She was taking washing jobs in the area and had been doing a Mrs Haywood's washing at Marsh Lane, then the following day was to wash and clean out her old house for Martha Hardwick at Lightwood (the two small villages virtually run into each other) the house that Ben had vacated after she left him. The Hardwick's owned the property and gave Eliza the key. Ben did not come to the house, which he would have done if Eliza wasn't there by someone else's say-so. Eliza started work washing the house and continued all day.

Ben showed up in area around half past one in the afternoon, and a lethal game of cat and mouse that ended badly for both stalker and stalked began, with Eliza aware of the fact that Ben was watching her, and Ben moving from house to house nearby, spying on her from neighbours' windows and commenting on her doings and what he intended – or was minded – to do. Ben went first to the house of Emily Cobb and asked if she had seen Eliza as he had asked her to do, and if Eliza had given Emily the bills he had to pay. Emily said, 'I told him what she had said, and he replied, "Then the —— may pay them herself." ' (4) Irritated, Ben then moved on.

He called next, around half-past three, at the house of a neighbour, Charles Brook, an ironstone miner who lived with his wife Sarah, and their three-year-old son. Sarah was twenty-two, close in age to Eliza, and very much in sympathy with her, and did not want Ben there. She did not care for him, like most of the woman in the villages around, and she told him she didn't want him in her house. He had a poaching friend, George Rollitt, who lodged at the house also, and this seems to have given him a familiarity and liberty in the house, for he quite brazenly confided that he had come to use her house to spy on Eliza:

'I told him I would rather he did not come there, and he said he would be b—— if he would not, if it was only to aggravate Eliza.' (7)

There was another reason, perhaps, why Ben chose the Brooks' house to spy on Eliza, for she saw him clearly at the window, and confided in a friend that "He is trying to aggravate me, but I won't speak to him whatever I do." (10) Ben wanted her to see him.

There does seem to have been some game going on between the pair of them, for although Sarah Brook was in sympathy with Eliza, and did not like Benjamin being at her house, Eliza had expressed jealousy of Sarah at one time, and as a paper reported:

'That his intention really was to excite her anger would seem to be borne out by the circumstance that in the afternoon he took tea at the house of a friend, of whose wife the deceased had expressed considerable jealousy.' (10)

For her part, Eliza went twice to John Barber's house, although she stayed only a few minutes, and of course, Ben was very jealous of Barber, believing he had had an affair with Eliza, though there was no evidence ever produced that this was so. Was Eliza doing it in the full knowledge that Ben could see her and was she doing it to 'wind him up' just as he might have been by going to Susan's house, because he knew that would make Eliza jealous? It certainly succeeded, if that was her plan, for Susan Brook said on the first occasion Ben looked confused, and the second time she went past to Barbers, he said, "There goes the b—— again." (10) Susan's husband had just come home, and she had made tea for them all, reluctantly offering Ben some, which he refused. Ben's language upset her, and she told him that she would not have such language used in her house, and Ben finally left, ordered out of the house, at six in the evening, having stood at the Brooke's window for two and a half hours. He probably made both the Brookes uneasy, for they testified at the inquest that as he was leaving, Charles Brooke told him to 'go and get some work,' to which Ben ominously replied that he would not do any more work in the country.' (7)

Everyone was offering Ben the same advice: get some work, pay your bills, stay out of trouble. But Ben wasn't listening. He was fixated on Eliza. He seemed almost cheerful at the coming confrontation he was planning as he drew his snare tight upon the trapped woman, for Sarah testified that 'The accused had been whistling and singing all the afternoon, and looked through the window towards the house where his wife was working. He did not make any threats whilst he was in the house, and seemed more cheerful than I have ever seen him before.' (8)

Ben called at another house, where lived Emily Cobb, another of Eliza's friends, but did not stay long, and then went on towards the George Inn. No one testified to him drinking there, but he did loiter around a Mrs. Gleadall's shop where he talked to some acquaintances, including his poaching friend George Rollit. He left them, saying that he was on his way over to Hundow Colliery 'to seek a job.' (7), but that was obviously a lie, for he had told Charles Brooke that he would never work again. He did not want to admit that he was on his way to ambush Eliza, or someone might have thwarted his plan in some way. A witness called Herbert Pendleton who had joined the men later testified that he saw Eliza in the distance and said that Ben must have seen her too, the inference being that Ben was in a hurry to get away and catch Eliza on her own in the fields between Lightwood and Handley.

*   *   *   *   *

Eliza finished her work and called on Mrs. Hardwick at around seven o'clock. She had worked hard all day, and even the *Derbyshire Times*, which seemed, strangely, to have much sympathy for Ben reported so, saying, 'Whatever faults the murdered woman may have had – and she had some, it could not be said that she was idle, for the residents all bear testimony to her hard working disposition.' (3) The paper added that she had been relatively cheerful and looking forward to a trip she was supposed to be taking to Sheffield the next day.

That day wouldn't dawn for Eliza, for having seen that Emily was nearly finished with her her work and would have to walk home soon, her stalker was already moving in on a spot where he knew she would be isolated and trapped. Leaving his friends, Ben headed to where Eliza would have to pass on her way to her parents' home. Before she left, Mrs Hardwick gave Eliza an old dress, a coal hammer and an earthenware bottle, which it is believed Ben had left when he gave up the house.

Eliza met a friend on her way, Jane Evans, who bid her goodnight, and saw that she had tears in her eyes. The last person she met before her killer was encountered shortly after, a young woman called Elizabeth Coe, the daughter of John Barber.

Elizabeth knew well the awful life that her friend had with Ben Hudson, for she had gone with Eliza a year ago to Eckington to take out a warrant against Ben. Although she was going in the opposite direction to Eliza, she consented when Eliza begged her to walk a little way back with her. Elizabeth said she walked back for a hundred yards with the frightened woman who told her that 'she was going on very badly, and was afraid and did not know what to do… she was in very low spirits.' (11) Despite all this, Elizabeth left her friend Eliza to walk on alone to her death.

A man called George Gosling came upon Ben in the fields through which Eliza must pass. He turned a sharp corner in the field and found Ben, who was loitering by a style. Gosling told the Crown Court later: 'I said, "Hey, Ben, what are tha doin' here?" and he replied, "I'm going to see your gaffers about a job." ' (11) He was referring to the colliery at Hundlow; George said he had heard there were no vacancies, and Ben turned away saying he would go the next day. In reality, what he was doing was occupying a strategic spot, for he would see Eliza whichever of the two possible routes she could take over the fields or down a lane, and it is quite likely that by then he could see Eliza heading his way and wanted to spring the trap. Eliza, for her part, had the setting sun in her eyes as it neared dusk, and would not see so well. No one knows which way she took exactly, but at a certain point she had to either cross a stile or pass it, and it is believed that Ben Hudson, certain of her route, hid himself on the opposite side of the hedge and waited for his estranged wife there.

About half an hour after he had encountered Hudson, Gosling returned by the same path, coming along the footpath which for a short length came along the green lane called Bowman Lane until he reached the stile which would take him over the field, cutting off a corner, to Lightwood. As he stepped up onto the stile, he could see lying in the field a broken bottle and a small hammer, 'like a coal hammer,' lying on the ground beyond. Gosling took up a stand on the stile to look around and saw the feet and petticoats of a girl or woman lying further on, the rest of her body being hidden by the hedge. Gosling walked back about 150 yards to a neighbour, blacksmith Charles Evans, who was in his garden, and asked him if he had heard anything. Evans had been in his garden for a couple of hours and had stopped work because of the fading light. He had heard no cries or commotion of any sort and walked back with Gosling to investigate.

In the dusk they could see the body of a young woman lying in the grass, about ten yards from where Ben Hudson had been seen standing earlier by Gosling. She was lying face up, her right hand on her left breast. Her face, Evans said, was badly cut and bruised, and a wound on her chin was still bleeding. Evans was bent low over her and later testified 'I scarcely knew where I was,' (11) Unsure of what do to do, he said, "Hullo?" even though he later said he was sure the poor woman before him was dead. Getting no response, Evans and Gosling went on to the Devonshire Arms and brought back the landlord, a Mr. Cowley, and some other people to view the awful scene. Everyone looked at the body, but no one recognised who it was. Given that it was nearly dark and there was a lot of bleeding and bruising to the dead woman's face, perhaps that is not surprising. A hedge stake was found which was presumed to be the murder weapon. It was lying about ten yards from the body and was about five feet in length, broken in four pieces, and covered in blood. Someone else found two teeth on the ground and picked them up as evidence. Witnesses observed that there was no evidence of a struggle on the ground around the body, although there was a depression where the head had been driven into the ground with the savagery of the assault, and there was a lot of blood on the ground.

Gosling and some others waited by the body whilst others went to fetch the nearest police officer, P.C. Alfred Hukin, from Barrow Hill, three miles away.

*   *   *   *   *

Ben Hudson's behaviour after killing his wife was bizarre. Leaving his wife dead or close to death, he made his way to West Handley, to the house of John Hudson, an uncle of both Ben and Eliza. John was only thirty-seven and seems to have been a confidant of Ben's, along with his wife Elizabeth, who was thirty-one. They had five children, so it must have been a full and cosy domestic setting that Ben intruded on at about half-past eight that night. Entering John's house, Ben shook hands with John and said dramatically, ' "Goodbye, this is the last time. I'm going to hang myself." ' (7) Leaving John Hudson aghast, Ben then went to a neighbour's house, a Jack Croft by name, where he once again wanted to shake hands, telling Crofts "Shake hands, old lad. I'm going." (2) When Crofts asked him where he was going, Ben replied, "To a better world than this, I hope." (7) and told Crofts he had 'knocked his wife's skull in, and intended to hang himself.' (7) Crofts could see how agitated Ben was and said "Sit thee down," but Ben said, "Nay, by …. I must be going. Give my respects to all." ' (2) Still seeming to revel in the drama and shock he was generating, Ben returned to his uncle's house and before John Hudson could sit down, he was back, wanting to shake hands with his aunt, who refused to do so until he told her what was wrong. Ben said "Nothing." John Hudson testified at the inquest that: 'She said, "There must be something amiss. I won't shake hands until you have told me." He then said, "I have broke the b—'s skull and I am going to hang myself this minute." She said, "Nay, thar wain't," and made an attempt to stop him, but he sprang out of her arms and stepped down the garden.' (2) Near the bottom of the garden Ben turned and said, "Remember me to all my friends and my sister Ann. Never mind that man that has won all the money." (7) That was believed to be a reference to his brother, whom he did not like, and who had won some money gambling recently. He then jumped the wall, and, witnesses reported that he was heard whistling and singing as he headed for some nearby woods, where he had intimated that he was going to hang himself.

People gathered to discuss the happenings, and no one seemed to know what to do, or to make of the whole affair, and the general crowd of neighbours all gathered at the nearby house of George Coupe, yet another uncle of Ben's, with whom he had been staying for at least some of the time since separating from Eliza. It appears that Ben had not gone there straight after the murder as he was not sure what kind of reception he would have received. Maybe, as he was without funds, he had worn his welcome out.

Ben had gone down to either nearby Stubbin Wood or Binkley Wood, but he had no intention of hanging himself; there was too much attention to bask in, and shortly after he returned to the street outside George Coupe's house where he boasted to some more villagers of breaking his wife's skull. One Scottish newspaper correspondent dourly summed up Ben's grandstanding by commenting pithily, 'Hudson appears to have made considerable ceremony over hanging himself, which was not altogether excused by the value of his existence.' (12)

After a while, Ben approached the door of his uncle George's house. He was a little uncertain of his welcome; he had been lodging there for part of the time at least after Eliza had left him and the tenancy of their own house had been given up. Penniless, and obsessed by plans of revenge as Ben was, he must have been a trial to his uncle and aunt. But he began to feel cold, and had not eaten all day, so was driven indoors by his needs, and possibly, an audience, for he seems to have felt no shame telling everyone he met what he had done, displaying instead something akin to a defiant pride. He didn't get the best of receptions. Most of the people in the room seem to have been related to each other, and related to both the murdered woman and the murderer, so that, shocked as they were by the death of Eliza, they also felt a duty towards Ben, but did not fail to let him know how they felt.

Ben leant in the doorway and said, "How are you going altogether?" John Hudson, uncle of both Ben and Eliza, said with the brutal frankness colliers were known for, "I thought thou had been hanged by now." (4) Ben replied, ' "I took a fresh thought. I want to see my uncle George, and I thought he would want to see me. I have come to 'liver myself up like a man to the policeman" ' (13) His uncle George Coupe made it clear that he didn't particularly want Ben inside his house, telling people around him that he would prefer Ben to stay outside, as he didn't want Ben to be taken by the police from his house when they came for him. Ben stayed outside for twenty minutes or so, but he complained that his feet were cold and was brought in and sat by the fire. He asked his aunty for some 'snap' (food), and she gave him two slices of bread and preserve, which he ate, leaving just the crust, as calmly as if he had just been for an evening walk in the fields.

It could be that Ben's nonchalance over his deed was irking uncle John Hudson, for he said to Ben as he sat down, "I think the best thing for thee will be to begin and prepare thyself for another world."(7) and other people repeated it to him in agreement. John then asked Ben where he would like to be buried, presumably after his trial, and Ben said, "At Handley." His uncle told him bluntly, "They'll not bury thee at Handley if they hang thee." (7) The law at that time required a person to be buried in an unmarked grave within the grounds of the gaol where he or she had been hanged. George Coupe's son Benjamin, trying to make sense of it all, mentioned to Ben Hudson that he had heard a pick and hammer had been found (he meant the coal hammer and stone bottle or jar), and Ben replied calmly, "I have not had them. I killed the b— with a hedge stake." (7) It was then noticed that there was blood on Ben's hands and face, and some on the corner of his neckerchief. Ben washed his hands and face clean of the blood and sat down to wait for the policeman in a room packed with relatives and acquaintances, much noise, confusion and crying ensuing. By all accounts he seems the only calm one there.

* * * * *

Constable Hukin, who had been fetched from Staveley, had viewed Eliza's beaten body in situ and taken notes, He got assistance in taking the body to the Devonshire Arms, where it was laid on a table ready for the inquest. He enquired of the local men where to find the self-confessed murderer and was shown to George Coupe's house at West Handley by Charles Evans. He arrived about ten in the evening and found Ben Hudson sitting in a chair by the fire. At first, Hukins thought John Hudson was the man he wanted but Ben said to the constable that he was the man he wanted. The policeman asked Ben if he had seen his wife that night, and at what time.

"Never mind, it matters now't to thee, I'm t'man," (7) Hudson calmly replied. At this, Hukin pulled out his handcuffs and Ben offered up his wrists with no sign of resistance to his fate.

It was just then that George Hudson, Eliza's brother, who had just learned of the killing of his sister, came into the crowded room and confronted his cousin.

"B— thy b— heart, I should like to have two rounds with thee," (13) he said to Benjamin, who received the threat coolly.

"Thou should have come a bit sooner," Ben replied. "I could

have finished thee in ten minutes, and if the police will allow me ten minutes now, I'll go and fight thee ten minutes."(13) It seems remarkable that George Hudson hadn't more concern for his sister while she was alive, but he stood back and allowed the officer to take away his captive.

As soon as they were clear of the crowd around Coupe's house, Hukins administered a charge of arrest on Ben, saying, "I charge you with violently assaulting your wife, so as to cause her death," and Ben answered, "I am guilty, I did it"' (2) Charles Evans, who was one of the first men to discover Eliza's body was due at work at the colliery where he worked and accompanied Ben and the constable across the fields towards Staveley as his house lay in that direction. Curiosity overcame him, and he asked:

' "Ben, whatever possessed thee to do a thing like as thou hast done now?" He replied callously, with all the lack of concern of a true psychopath: "Well, it was her own bringing on. I met her at the stile and asked her a few questions, but she would not give me a straight-forward answer, so I thought I would straighten her." (14)

Charles Evans pressed on with his questions. He was puzzled by the fact that he had heard no cries for help or screams of pain from the woman being murdered, even though he had been in his garden not far away.

"No," Ben said. "I stopped her from that at first." (14) As far as he was concerned, it was all Eliza's fault for not answering him correctly, and she deserved her 'punishment' from him. He had 'straightened' her, and that was that.

Ben was locked in a police cell and was visited every ten minutes or so, until four in the morning when it was daylight and a Sergeant Hallam took Ben to Chesterfield Police Station where he was charged with 'killing and slaying' his wife, Presumably the 'slaying' (legally defined as violent killing) element of the charge was in reference to the violent nature of the crime, in case his legal defence was later to be that of manslaughter.

Word of the killing spread rapidly among the mining communities of North East Derbyshire, and there was a lot of bad feeling towards Ben Hudson, not only for the deed, but for the lack of any

160

remorse shown afterwards. Local and national papers relayed the gruesome details and Hudson's glorying in it. It is lucky for Ben that the authorities chose not to bring the accused man to the inquest, although it was usually the norm, for when it convened at the School Rooms in Middle Handley at 4.00 pm on Friday, after the fifteen-man jury had viewed the body at the Devonshire Arms, where it was laid out on a large table, there were a number of miners in the assembly who had come purposely with the intention of lynching him. The inquest heard enough of Ben's prior actions and his confession afterwards which was more of a boast to anyone who would listen to harden hearts further and cement public opinion.

There might have been more at play than merely avenging an ill-used woman, however, for Ben had brought disgrace on both the community of Handley and the wider coal-mining communities around. Several scathing indictments of colliers and their ways began to appear in publications which dealt with the murder, and the anger towards Ben grew. One early report, quoted at the beginning of this account, condemned the whole community as 'foul-mouthed colliers', and 'barbaric' and 'ignorant', speaking of a 'social sore' and concluding: '…how vast does the work of elevating, instructing, and Christianising them appear.' (2) Another newspaper concluded their report by saying 'Such is collier life in England.' (12) There were many other similar blanket condemnations, and it rankled in the colliery villages and towns of the area. They were tough people, sturdy country stock absorbed into the new industries which had arisen in the area, and were harshened, maybe, by the hard life they had to lead to earn their pay, but it angered them that they were all being tarred with the same brush.

A letter was sent to the *Sheffield Independent* which had so slandered the people of Handley. It was from a W.E. Helm of the Church Handley Schools, and in it he protested strongly against the attack on his community by the paper, saying acidly that because a crime was committed in an area 'did not prove the whole of the inhabitants be steeped in barbarism. If so, Sheffield would not stand high in the scale of civilization.' (15) Mr. Helm declared that Handley was peaceful and well-ordered, that violence was rarely known and that 'Respectable people, who have lived here for many years, do not even remember a fight,' and that 'the effect of the crime on the population was to simply to stun and to paralyze.' (15) The hasty generalisation of the newspaper, he said, had made the whole population of the area seem 'ruffianly and brutal' (15), and he concluded by saying that if as the paper said, the work of elevating and Christianising the colliery communities was vast it was strange that some authorities were attempting to exclude religious teaching from the state schools. It was a masterly admonition from someone who knew the area well.

After hearing several witnesses the inquest was adjourned until the following Wednesday for a full postmortem to be conducted, and further evidence to be gathered.

Eliza's body was released to her family for burial, and a paper reported that a strange custom prevalent in North Derbyshire, 'at least among the working classes' (16) as the *Derby Mercury* primly reported, of allowing anyone to view the corpse and pay their respects, was observed, and on the Sunday, the day of the funeral, over a thousand people filed through a room in her parents' house to see Eliza, laid out in readiness for the funeral to follow. Thousands visited the village that day, drawn by a ghoulish interest, to view the grave and were also drawn to the scene of the murder, where Eliza's blood could still be seen 'and the marks of the prisoner's feet being as distinct as they were three days ago.' (16)

The funeral took place on the Sunday, 27th April. It was a simple, country funeral, the mourners on foot and the coffin being borne by four young men, who carried it the half-mile from Eliza's parents' house to the church at Middle Handley. Eight young women held the pall (a mourning canopy) over the coffin and 'upwards of two thousand persons witnessed the last sad rites,' (17) most people arriving an hour before time and lining the route each side of the road. The coffin was 'followed by the aged father of the deceased, who seemed greatly distressed, the two children of the murderer and his victim (so young that they were scarcely able to keep up with the procession), by two sisters and two brothers of the deceased, and by other relatives.' (7) Eliza's mother does not seem to have attended the funeral, for she isn't mentioned as present and some papers reported that she had been very ill since the murder, being '… almost heartbroken… subject to fainting and hysteria, and has shown symptoms of serious illness.' (8) The Rev. Darrington met the cortege at the entrance to the church and officiated. 'As the coffin was lowered into the grave a wreath and a cross of beautiful flowers were placed upon it. At the conclusion of the service, it was with difficulty that some of the relatives could be induced to leave the grave.' (17)

If many were mourning Eliza's death, her husband certainly wasn't, and showed little concern when he was brought up before a magistrate at the office of the magistrate's clerk the following day, Monday 28th April. He was brought in a cab to the gate of the building, watched by a large crowd, and trouble was expected. The crowd, however, was silent and well-behaved. Ben acted in an astonishing manner. He was laughing as he alighted from the cab, and he laughed and chatted with the police and other prisoner's in the ante-room. 'In fact, he treated the whole matter with perfect indifference.' (2) Given that he was usually described by most people as surly and generally uncommunicative, he was probably putting on an act of bravado, but it didn't seem to have gone down well with the crowd outside, for when he came back out, after being charged and having nothing to say in response, the assembled onlookers, which included a good proportion of women, 'raised a cry of execration. The prisoner responded by raising his manacled wrists above his head and clapping his hands. There were cries of "Turn the cab over!" but no one made the attempt, and he was driven away amid the shouts of the crowd.' (2) The correspondent for the *Derbyshire Times* was expecting to see a monster in Ben Hudson, but was surprised that such psychopaths appear normal:

'He is about the average height, and well, but not stoutly, built, and betrays in his countenance little of that brutality of that disposition which is attributed to him.' (7)

* * * * *

The inquest, which had been adjourned, was resumed and completed on the Wednesday, in the school room at Middle Handley before the coroner, a Mr. C.S.B. Busby and a jury of twelve men. There was also a police presence, comprising the Deputy Chief Constable Lawson, Superintendent Oldham, Detective Inspector Davis, and Sergeant Hallam. The first witness examined was Mr. Court, physician and surgeon of Staveley, who had conducted the postmortem after the preliminary inquest.

The doctor testified that he had examined the body at the Devonshire Arms. He found the face covered with blood, and the hair matted with blood, and with thorns sticking in the back part of the head. He found six wounds to the face and the cheek bone was broken and lay loose inside one wound. The wounds were all lacerated ones and would have bled heavily. The jawbone was fractured, and the front teeth had been smashed off. Both eyelids were blackened and swollen shut. Beneath the scalp there was a great deal of bleeding to both temples, but Court found no damage to the brain, and all the vital organs were healthy. There were cuts to the chin and the branches to the jugular vein were torn across. There were superficial wounds to the arms and bruising. The doctor gave it as his opinion that the deceased had bled to death, and had probably been unconscious after the first blow, delivered while she was standing up, and that death had taken about half an hour.

It was clear from the doctor's findings that it was a frenzied killing. Ben had concentrated on the head alone, with such ferocity that she was unrecognizable by the local people who were fetched from the Devonshire Arms by Evans and Gosling. Such was the ferocity of the attack that, although the skull wasn't fractured, Hudson succeeded in breaking the hedge stake into three or four (accounts vary) pieces, and this stake had been made from the spliced branch of an oak tree, very hard wood indeed.

Doctor Court gave it as his opinion that death was caused by loss of blood from the cuts on the face and chin. Some of the cuts, he said, may have been caused by fragments from the stone bottle Eliza had been carrying. He did not think that immediate medical attention would have saved her life.

There were two surprises in the inquest. The first sad fact was that Doctor Court divulged that Eliza had been at an early stage of pregnancy, about six weeks, so that in killing his own wife, Hudson killed his own child as well. The second was a touching little detail that the papers made much of.

When Eliza's corpse was undressed to examine it, found in the left bosom of her stays was a leather purse. It contained an eardrop, a button, a small amount of money in coinage amounting to seven shillings and tenpence-halfpenny (approximately 39p), a packet of pins, and a piece of paper with this charm written upon it:

> "It is not these pins I meant to burn,
> But Ben Hudson's heart I mean to turn,
> Let him neither eat, speak, drink, nor comfort find
> Till he comes to me and speaks his mind." (7)

This 'pin magic' was quite common among country folk in England, even as late as the nineteenth century, and usually involved sticking pins in a burning candle and reciting a verse similar to the one found on Eliza's body. The belief was that by the time the candle had burnt down to the pins the errant lover (usually male) would think of the one working the love-spell and come to them. Whoever had written the spell out for Eliza is not named, for both she and Ben were illiterate, unable even to sign to the agreement at Eckington with anything more than a cross against their names. What seems inexplicable is why Eliza still had the love charm. Had she forgotten that it still lay there in her purse, or was she still, secretly, in love with such a beast who so ill-used her? The latter doesn't seem likely since she had told everyone that she was determined to break free of Ben this time. One paper summed up the grisly irony of the sad little package very well indeed:

'Foolish paper, and too faithful wife! He did come to her; but it was not in the sense of her silly yearning bit of village magic, and the "mind" that he spoke was brutal, bloody, and beyond all softening.'(18)

Following on after the doctor, other witnesses gave evidence as to the events leading up to the murder, and Ben's behaviour and statements he made afterwards. The inquest being so thorough, with so many witnesses it was then adjourned to the next day. The following day further witnesses were called.

A chilling piece of evidence given by the arresting officer, P.C.

Alfred Hukin, showed the violence meted out by Hudson to his defenceless wife. He told the magistrate about the scene of the murder. He said that, 'there was blood near the stile, and there was a deal of blood in the place where the head of the deceased lay. There was a round hole not far from the stile; it was about the size of a basin top.' The coroner asked, 'Can you form any idea how the hole was made?' and Hukins answered, grimly matter-of-fact, 'It appeared to me as if the head of the deceased had been hammered into the ground by blows.' (19)

Eventually the Coroner began to sum up. During his remarks to the jury, the Coroner decided to recall Gosling to testify as to where he had come upon Hudson lurking before the murder. Gosling told the assembly that it was no more than three yards from where the body was later found. There was no further evidence needed for the Coroner to advise the jury '... that on the facts as laid before them he thought they could not avoid returning a verdict of wilful murder against Benjamin Hudson.'(7) It took the jury just three minutes to agree with the Coroner and return that very verdict. Ben would go on trial for wilful murder.

*   *   *   *   *

The *Derbyshire Times* now weighed in on the case, tarring in an editorial the whole community of Handley with the same brush. They called for a 'missionary enterprise' to a place not:

> 'Where the feathery palm trees rise,
> And the date grows ripe under sunny skies.' (7)

The writer of the article fulminated that there were few temples to alien gods 'in the district we refer to, except those of Bacchus.... yet for the absolute heathenism of a part of the inhabitants we may fairly compare them to a savage tribe... The marriage tie... appears to be almost ignored at Handley.' (7) The instance of Hibbert attempting to buy Eliza back from Ben for a sovereign was cited, as was the fact that both Ben and two of Eliza's children were born out of wedlock. The article further attacked the 'domestic morality of the class to which Hudson belonged,' the illiteracy among the miners, and 'the language of the man was of the lowest description, as we are sorry to say is too often the case among colliers' (7) The fact that Ben was a poacher and amused himself with rabbit coursing was also an indicator of 'the character of the class to which Hudson and his victim belonged.' (7) The editor dipped his pen finally in vitriol and righteously concluded: '…if the Home Missionary Society want a new field of labour let them send a missionary or two to Handley.' (7)

Up and down the land, other newspapers weighed in on 'the collier' as a class, with scant regard for the truth of the Handley case. The truth was that the coalminer was often vilified by the middle and upper classes, one historian writing that 'The image of the miner was of a man ignorant, violent, besotted with drink, and isolated from all humanizing influences.'(20) Part of the reason for the wholesale condemnation was that the coalminer didn't fit in with the rigid social control that the Victorian ruling classes tried to enforce, and his independence and often lack of respect for his 'betters' irked them. Far from being some form of brute beast, the collier was a highly skilled man, practising with skill the art of getting coal whilst preserving his own life and that of his fellow workers: knowing how far to undercut a coalface, where to place props, how to detect invisible gas, listening for the many danger sounds within a mine, how deep to drill a powder charge… 'All of these were skills which place the nineteenth century collier into the ranks of the labour aristocracy.' (20) Coalminers, too, were an emerging political force at a time when working men had few rights. Relying on each other for their lives below surface and living in close communities, they formed strong social bonds. Frequently exploited by pit owners, they organised strikes, formed unions, and reminded many in power in Britain of revolutionaries close to home in Europe, who had unseated politicians and wealthy landowners. The collier frightened his betters; the miners hewed King Coal, as it was called, and the vital fuel powered and drove the Industrial Revolution, and, hating their dependence on the collier, those who exploited him, also condemned him. It was a strange relationship.

One lone voice protested to the *Derbyshire Times*, it seems, about the slander of Handley residents. It was from R.W Crawshaw, 'an old inhabitant of the Handley area', (21) who lived at The Hagge, a Jacobean manor house and farm at Nether Handley. He was aggrieved that because there were 'one or two black sheep' in Handley, the whole population was unjustly condemned. He pointed out that there was only one 'Temple to Bacchus,' the Devonshire Arms, and that was 'a remarkably well conducted one,' and that 'the people (of Handley) are as quiet, well conducted, and respectable as any in the county' (21) He got short shrift from the editor of the *Derbyshire Times*, who stuck to his guns and his prejudices, saying that the readers of the paper should consider the facts as sworn to in the evidence given at the inquest and then decide for themselves whether 'Mr Crawshaw can maintain his proposition that the Handley people are "as well conducted and respectable as any in the county." Certainly, if old fashioned prejudices in favour of chastity and virtue in man and woman are to be the test we must join issue with him in toto.' (21) So, having besmirched a whole community on the basis of the conduct of one psychotic man and one woman who fell pregnant outside of marriage, which was very common in many communities of the time, as anyone who has examined parish records can attest to, the editor maintained his bigoted view.

*　*　*　*　*

Ben seemed indifferent to the position he was in. On his way to Derby Goal he had kept up an air of bravado, as if he had performed some sort of justifiable and heroic act, and in his first week of confinement he spoke little to his gaolers. He seemed little concerned about the position he was in. His captors reported that his appetite was good but that he was 'moody and reticent' (22) when spoken to. That would seem to have been his nature, however, as others who knew him had spoken to the same attitude on Ben's part.

The following week Ben was again brought back to Chesterfield to a Magistrates Court. It had originally been planned to take place on Monday but was changed for some reason to the following day. A large crowd had assembled outside and waited for hours, some to look on, others with a real feeling of animosity, and they endured heavy rain for hours until they were convinced they wouldn't see Hudson until the following day. When he did come the authorities were so concerned that there might be a 'scene' at Chesterfield Station that Ben was taken off the train along with Mr. Sims, governor of Derby Goal, under police guard at Clay Cross station, one stop before Chesterfield, then brought to the court in a cab.

A considerable number of Ben's family was there, some to give evidence, some to support him, including Ben's brother, who "burst into tears, and his other relatives seemed much distressed.' (22) Ben seemed to be disconcerted by the emotions but 'quickly recovered his composure.' (22) It was noted by one reporter that Ben's 'air of bravado' he had shown in court the week before was gone. Other locals were there also, mainly to give evidence before the magistrate, and there were so many that nearly all the public benches were utilised for their seating. The evidence was more or less the same as that given at the inquest, with the exception of the testimony of a man called William Robinson, who said that in 1869 he had been employed by the farmer who owned the field Eliza was killed in. He had done repairs to a fence next to the stile, and had put in two stoops, rails, and a stake, all made of oak. They had still been in place when he passed four days before the murder, but when he passed two days after it, he noticed the stake had gone. He examined the stake Ben had killed Eliza with and thought it was the same one, 'but could not swear to it.' (22)

The evidence being given, the magistrate then formally committed Ben to the next County Assizes. Ben seemed unperturbed by the news. His brother had brought in refreshments for Ben, and Ben stood forward to the rail of the dock to hear he would be committed to the Assizes 'with a huge sandwich in one hand and a mug of tea in the other'! (5) When the relatives left court there were tears again, and his mother and brother and some of the Handley locals shook Ben's hand as they bid farewell, even some of the witnesses who had given evidence against him.

But not everyone viewed Ben as tolerantly. People continued to read and talk about him, and public feeling was high. Many continued to visit the murder spot and talk about the awful deed. Some were angry for the awful, cowardly murder of a defenceless women, others were incensed that Ben Hudson had brought such disgrace on the mining class, who were reviled for the sin of one man, and the *Sheffield Independent* claimed that 'deep execrations are uttered against the husband murderer.' (8) Such a crowd had gathered outside the hall during and after the hearing, all waiting for Ben Hudson, that it wasn't considered safe to take Ben out to put in a waiting cab and take him to the railway station, so he was held back until six while the situation was considered. Threats had been made against his life a fortnight earlier and opinion had hardened in that time. Eventually a clever stratagem was devised:

'The private entrance to the hall is in a large yard, and as soon as a cab was brought there the crowd rushed into the yard and stood as near to the entrance as they could. A number of police cleared a pathway to the cab and took up positions to keep the people back. Two policemen then went and quietly closed the gates, shutting the crowd in the yard. At the same moment the prisoner was hurried out at the front gates to a cab in the street and driven away almost before the crowd had discovered how they had been misled. They appeared rather to enjoy the joke than otherwise.' (22) The cab then continued to Clay Cross railway station to evade any demonstrations, from where Hudson was taken to Derby Goal.

As to the other victims in this case, Eliza's children, Mary, aged six, and George, four years old, a subscription fund was got up for them, with frequent advertisements in the papers, and quite a good sum was raised to ensure their welfare. Eliza's father applied for wardship of the two infants but was refused by the Chesterfield Board of Guardians who had authority over care for orphans. 'It was the unanimous opinion of the board, from his admissions before the coroner at the inquest on the body of his daughter, that Hudson was anything but a proper person to be the guardian of the children.' (23) They were temporarily taken into the workhouse while it was seen how much was raised, and a respectable person could be found to foster them.

It was a long wait for the Assizes, but Ben endured it placidly. He could neither read nor write, and conversed little with his gaolers, though he replied if spoken to. That seemed to be his general manner, uncommunicative, bordering on surly, and from his general behaviour apart from the murder, one is entitled to ask if Ben was of very low intellect, or, indeed, 'not quite the ticket', as the miners used to term it. His lack of concern at his plight seems to suggest it, along with other indicators.

*   *   *   *   *

Ben finally came to trial on Tuesday July 15th, 1873 in Crown Court at Derby. There was a great interest in the case and as soon as the doors were opened there was a rush for seats. 'The lower floor reserved for the public, was quickly filled, and the galleries were crowded for the most part with ladies.' (11) Ben was calm and quiet when brought into the dock, showing none of his earlier bravado, a correspondent noted, adding that he seemed paler (not surprising, since he had been confined to a cell for two months), and 'had a decidedly weary air as he leaned with physical listlessness against the handrail with his hands folded…'(9) He was represented in court by a Mr. Waddy, a Mr. Buszard and a Mr. Kennedy appeared for the prosecution. Justice Honyman was the judge

As the trial began, the charge was put to the defendant and he was asked how he pleaded, and, astonishingly, Ben answered 'Guilty', possibly another indicator that he was not particularly bright. His defence solicitor, who it seems was only instructed in the case quite recently, probably the day before, immediately came to the rescue. Mr Waddy said that it was a mistake, that his client thought 'that he was asked whether he had been the cause of his wife's death, but not of malice aforethought.' (11) Waddy was clearly going to try and get his client off on a lighter, non-capital charge, since by his own admission and all evidence offered, Ben had killed Eliza. The charge was put again, and this time Ben replied, 'with great distinctness of tone, "Not Guilty, my lord."' (11)

Waddy's extremely slim chance was to mitigate the crime committed by Hudson and achieve somehow a verdict of manslaughter. The judge ruled that the jury would 'practically have no doubt that the prisoner had caused the death of his wife.' (11) Buszard, in his opening remarks as prosecutor, said that he was not, after the judge's remarks, going to go into depth on the difference between murder and manslaughter, but he thought that the level of violence shown in the killing of Eliza Hudson that even if it had not been committed with the actual intention of causing death, there could be little doubt that it was a case of wilful murder. Ben had, at the least, intended causing serious injury to his wife, and in so doing, she had died. Buszard also submitted to the jury the evidence of the pins and love charm found upon Eliza, proof, he argued, that Eliza bore no *animus* against the prisoner and had not instigated the violence. He told the jury that it would therefore be for them to decide whether the violence had been deliberately inflicted and whether there had been some premeditation of the crime, 'and when they had done this it seemed to him that they would only have a sad and painful duty to perform, to say that he (Hudson) was guilty of the crime of wilful murder.' (11)

The first witness called by the prosecution was Richard Hudson, Eliza's father, and as he began to lay out for the jury the history of Ben and Eliza's stormy relationship, and the violence meted out towards her by Ben, Waddy rose to his feet and objected. His weak defence would be that the violence was not a habitual response on the part of Ben, but had arisen out of a 'sudden quarrel, which could not have arisen days before the occurrence took place.' (9) Clearly, he did not want it to be seen that the murder was the foreseeable result of a pattern of sustained violence which had increased in severity over the years.

Justice Honyman seems to have been stuck for a ruling to this objection, and the reason could have been that he was newly appointed to the Bench, having only been made a judge in January of that year. This was his first time of sitting in Derby, and although he was noted for being the best commercial lawyer of his day, with a tenacious memory, he does not seem to have been very experienced in adjudication of criminal law. He decided here that this was beyond his experience, and he retired briefly to consult with a colleague-judge, Baron Pollock, who was sitting in judgement on other cases in a nearby court. When Honyman returned he ruled that 'nothing ought to be admitted as evidence that constituted a previous offence, but if possible, confine it to recent occurrences.' (9) The problem here was that an accused is legally allowed to expect the jury be called to consider only the specific crime laid before them, and previous offences can only be submitted as evidence against them if the defendant or his counsel claims in court that he or she is of good character. Eliza's father had begun to disclose historic abuse, and may have disclosed that

Ben had been taken to court and imprisoned before for his violence to Eliza, but the judge ruled that this was not to be brought into the case if possible. It was a fine line that the prosecution walked here.

The trial was basically a shortened recounting of evidence already given by witnesses at the inquest and the hearing before the magistrates, but one item of evidence stands out as a possible reason for the last disagreement between Eliza and Benjamin, which caused her to leave him, and resulted in her death. This testimony was given by John Morton, a poaching friend of Ben's. Ben had called on him, and it seems they went out poaching, for Morton took a gun with him (he had bought it off Ben some time earlier), and they walked over from Lightwood to West Handley and back:

'On the 23rd April the prisoner came to my house… I talked with him about his wife, whom he said was "thick with other men.," The man Hibberd, he said, had been to him and offered him a sovereign for his wife, but he would neither let him or any one else have her. I had a gun with me, and he said if I would let him have it he would shoot his wife, and Hibberd too… Hibberd lived about a mile and a half from the prisoner, and was in the habit of going to his (Ben's) house. I saw him (going) to the house of the prisoner at eight o'clock on the night of Easter Monday. The prisoner was away from home at the time. I met him coming in an opposite direction about half an hour before I met the prisoner…' (24) According to John Morton, Hibberd told him that he had been to Eliza's house and 'was going to fetch her.'(9) Morton told the court he saw Hibberd and Eliza talking at her door for about ten minutes and this was about half an hour before Morton met up with Ben and discussed his wife. Just what Eliza was doing at her house door isn't clear, but it was about the time that her father fetched her back from Lightwood to live with at her parent's house, so she could have been waiting for him, or Richard Hudson was inside the house or at Martha Hardwick's, hearing of Ben's latest violent attacks on his daughter. Whatever Hibberd was doing was certainly not helping resolve the situation, as innocent as the act of talking to Eliza may have been.

It seems reasonable to assume that Morton would have told Ben what he had seen, and this would have incensed Ben further. Was Morton stirring up an already inflamed Ben, who was always terrifically jealous since his early youth of Eliza talking to anyone? Did Ben think that Eliza was making plans to finally have done with him and go and live with Hibberd? Hibberd had offered to buy her from Ben, and it seemed he may have been trying to persuade Eliza to go back to him.

The sale of a wife wasn't a thing unheard of in the countryside, even as late as 1873, and seems to have been quite accepted among country people at one time, the most famous incident of it being the fictional wife-sale in Thomas Hardy's *The Mayor of Casterbridge*. It is believed to have become an 'invented custom' in rural communities after The Marriage Act of 1753 made a marriage only legal if performed by a clergyman. Prior to that it was a rural tradition that a couple could agree to be a married couple, and this was looked upon as binding. Once the legal requirement to marry in the presence of clergy was enforced, and legal divorce became a requirement in order to remarry, a belief became widespread among countryfolk that a man could transfer his wife to another 'husband' by accepting a sum of money, and would often offer her in a public place, such as a market, frequently with a halter around her neck, and if the wife also agreed to both the sale and the buyer, it was seen as a legal transaction and a remarriage! It must be said that often the woman was as willing to accept the new partner, as they were known to each other, could not afford to go through a prohibitively expensive divorce, and that by paying some money to the former husband, some sort of legal acknowledgement of the new arrangement had been made. The past, as L.P. Hartley said, is another country. They did things differently.

So perhaps Hibberd approaching Ben with a sovereign was, in that time and place, the most sensible way out of the terrible fix both Ben and Eliza were in. Eliza, if she accepted the arrangement Hibberd seems to have been pressing her to, would go back to someone who cared about her and didn't beat her, and Ben would be free of any debts incurred by Eliza. But Ben seems to have been impervious to reason and set on destruction of both Eliza's life and his own. Morton's information set the tinder burning.

Why didn't Eliza accept Hibberd, because, surely, if she had listened to him, she would have gone to his house, not her father's, where she appears not to always have been welcome? At her father's there was little room for her and her children as well, and with Hibberd she would have been safe. There's no record left to say why she didn't accept Hibberd, but it could have been for a number of reasons. Perhaps she suspected she was pregnant again with, presumably, Ben's child, and was unable to tell Hibberd. Perhaps Hibberd wanted her, but not the children, or wouldn't take her unless Ben agreed. It could even be that she hoped against hope for a change of heart on Ben's part, for she still stuck to her sad little packet of pins and love charm that obviously wasn't working. We shall never know, but it would seem that Morton's tale-telling and Hibberd's interference caused Ben's temper and slighted ego to erupt in deadly violence – and sealed Eliza's doom.

*　　*　　*　　*　　*

Once the witnesses had again given their awful evidence (to which Ben had listened throughout the long day with not the slightest show of emotion and keeping his eyes always fixed firmly on the judge), Mr Buszard summed up for the prosecution. He said there could be no doubt that the prisoner had caused the death of 'the unfortunate woman'; (11) the only question that they had to consider was whether there were any circumstances which could reduce the charge from wilful murder to manslaughter. By law, the provocation had to be more than just words: actual violence had to have been committed against the accused. There was no evidence of this. Buszard looked at the fact that Eliza had illegitimate children before marrying Ben, but 'The accused had had made a marriage contract knowing well what her character was; and there was no concealment about her having these children.'(11) Buszard pointed out that the only time in such a case as Hudson's where a man could justifiably plead manslaughter was if he literally caught her in the act of adultery. Further, there need be no need to prove prolonged premeditation of the act which caused Eliza's death. It had been shown that Ben was loitering in the area where Eliza had to pass, that he 'had beaten her to death whilst labouring under no excitement, and looking at the weapon used and the results, he (Buszard) asked the jury whether they should have any doubt that the accused did not intend to kill his wife.' (11) It should be obvious, Buszard argued, that Hudson's determination in the commission of the deed and the terrible injuries inflicted upon Eliza pointed to a determination to kill her.

During the trial the defence attempted – and succeeded, partly – in painting Eliza's reputation as black as it could, claiming that Ben was provoked beyond reason to a sudden act of violence against his wife, that the meeting with Eliza that night was 'purely accidental, and that the accused was, whilst exasperated with her taunts and probably by her actions (for a hammer was in her possession) had taken her life in a sudden quarrel.' (11) The idea that Eliza, who was slightly built, had necessitated a well-built man to take a five-foot hedge stake of solid oak to defend himself, was a fairly desperate flight of fancy, so Mr. Waddy then fell back on a character assassination of Eliza. She was, he said, 'bad, false, ill-tempered, and evil.' (11) Her morality was attacked so that she was the sole architect of the circumstances which led to her bearing illegitimate children, even though Ben was the father of one, and, in a way, Eliza's death was divine punishment for her lust, for Waddy quoted the bible text (James 1:15), "That lust when it hath conceived bringeth forth sin, and sin when it is finished bringeth forth death." (11) Thus, in a way, Eliza deserved it all, and Ben was merely an instrument of God! So ran the argument, to Waddy's reasoning before the jury. Waddy explained to them that: 'The beginning of it was in the woman's vice (no mention of any other willing participants who conspired to get Eliza pregnant!) and in the woman's crime, until outraged and stung beyond the power of endurance, partly by her wickedness and infidelity, and her careless triumphant taunts, the accused imbrued his hands in her blood in the quarrel which took place.'(11) This, of course, was nonsensical hyperbole on Waddy's part, because at no time had any evidence been brought forward that Eliza was unfaithful to Ben while they were married, Eliza had committed no 'crime', as Waddy stated, and there was no evidence, even from Ben, who chose not to take the stand in his own defence, that Eliza had taunted him (Eliza knew better not to enrage her husband). Waddy made much of the fact that Ben had not taken a weapon to the meeting, and that the crime should therefore be considered as being manslaughter. He finally reminded the jurymen of their duty towards a 'fellow-countryman' and appealed that they find Benjamin Hudson guilty only of a lesser crime – manslaughter.

His Lordship then summed up, and he clearly had not been persuaded by Mr. Waddy that Ben had acted upon impulse, sorely tried by the behaviour of a culpable Jezebel of a wife. He pointed out that the injuries caused were the result of considerable violence, but that if the jury really believed that 'if they thought that what had been suggested by the defence had occurred, it was not murder but manslaughter… but the weight of evidence certainly went to prove that nothing of the sort had taken place between them.'(11)

And it was there that Mr. Waddy's frail flight of fancy came crashing down into the dust. The jury retired to consider their verdict and were back in about an hour.

'On being asked if they had considered their verdict, the foreman of the jury said, "We have my lord, and find the prisoner guilty of Wilful Murder; but, owing to the unhappy life he has passed with his wife, the jury wish to recommend him to the merciful consideration of the court."' (11) They meant for an appeal to be made for commutation of the death sentence, life imprisonment being the fairer sentence in their view. Again, there was a protest in court, though again we are not told whether for or against Ben Hudson: 'There was a marked demonstration amongst the occupants of the court whilst the foreman was delivering the verdict, but it was quickly supressed.' (11) One assumes that it was against Ben not paying for his horrible crime with his life. Someone in the public section of the court wanted to see Ben swing.

The Clerk of the Arraigns formally asked the prisoner why sentence of death should not be passed upon him, but Ben either seemed not to care, or, more likely, not understand what was happening. He showed 'a surprising amount of equanimity, (and) did not make any reply.' (11)

Justice Honyman bowed his head slightly as a court official placed the square of black cloth on his head. This was the 'black cap', based on Tudor court fashion, and which was traditionally placed over the judicial wig before sentence of death was pronounced. 'Amid the almost breathless silence of the Court, (he) proceeded to pass sentence of death on the prisoner.' (11)

Justice Honyman, 'whose emotion was so great that several times his voice was rendered inaudible by his own sobs,' told the condemned man: '…the jury, after a very patient trial, in which you have been ably defended by your counsel, have found you guilty of the wilful murder of your wife, a person whom of all others you ought to have cherished and protected. It is perfectly true that as the jury say, you have led a very unhappy life… but speaking for myself, I can hardly think that the way in which you and your wife lived together justified you, or afforded the slightest excuse, for taking her life under the circumstances you did. The punishment for the person who is guilty of wilful murder is death, and death only. I have no discretion in the matter. I will take care that the recommendation (of the jury for mercy) is forwarded to the proper quarter, where I have no doubt it will receive due consideration; but I think I should only be guilty of false kindness to you if I held out the slightest hope that your life will be spared. In the meantime I recommend you to spend in the best way you can the short time which remains to you.' (11) The customary sentence of death was then pronounced on Hudson.

The judge's emotional sobs seem strange when one looks at the brutality of the murder and, surely, the inevitable outcome of the trial, but Justice Honyman had only just been appointed to be a judge at the end of January of that year. He was notably a commercial lawyer, rated the best in the country, so perhaps this was the first murder case he had judged or even been involved in and the awful responsibility of pronouncing the sentence of death on a fellow human being was hard for him to accept.

* * * * *

Hudson was taken the short distance to Derby Gaol in Vernon Street to await execution. There he was confined in the condemned cell, and sat, unable to read or write, and making no conversation with the two warders who guarded him day and night. The warders reported that they often had to repeat a question before he would answer them, maintaining a 'sullen silence.' (26) His appetite, which had been so good during his pretrial imprisonment, waned as the execution day approached, but he made no mention of his wife, or any regret at first. He became bored with the routine, and on at least two occasions he told his gaolers that he wished the execution was over. He attended chapel each day along with the other prisoners and the prison chaplain visited him too and found him attentive. He was asked by the chaplain eventually if he regretted what he had done, and he is reported as saying that 'he felt sorry the moment he did the horrible deed.' (25) Given Ben's boastful behaviour after the murder, that should be taken with a pinch of salt. There were many who remembered Ben's boast that he had cracked Eliza's skull, finished the job, and was glad of it, and it is significant that there was no petition raised in the area where he had lived calling for a commutation of the sentence of death passed on Hudson. The chaplain to the High Sheriff, a Reverend Olivier, visited Ben in gaol on the Thursday, with a bare four days clear before the execution, and was, as one paper put it, 'so impressed with his (Ben's) condition, that he proceeded to London the following day and had an interview with the Home Secretary, to whom he made an appeal on the prisoner's behalf.' (26) Quite what he saw in Ben is not stated, but it cut no ice with Mr. Bruce, Home Secretary at the time, and he said he could accept any petition unless it were submitted in writing. Olivier hurried back to Derby and attempted to raise a petition, but with such a short time left, managed to get only a few signatories. Or maybe those petitioned recalled the savagery of the murder and were not keen to sign. The petition was forwarded to the Home Secretary urgently, but he did not find sufficient reason to recommend commutation of the death sentence. Mr. Olivier went on Sunday, the day before the execution, to tell Hudson there was no hope, and asked Ben if he was sorry for what he had done. Ben seems to have told the chaplain what he wanted to hear, or had a sudden conversion, which isn't unusual when a man is as close to death as he was, for he told Mr Olivier that 'he was sorry not only for the sin against his wife, but against God.' (26) He also made more of an excuse than a confession, for what he told the chaplain to the High Sheriff of Derbyshire was patently false. He said that he had not gone to the scene of the murder with the intention of killing Eliza, 'in fact he was not aware that he should meet her there,' (26) which was patently untrue, when one considers how he had hung around the area of Lightwood, observing Eliza for most of the day. He continued, 'the meeting was unexpected, but he began talking to her about "the children and bills, and one word led to another" (26) until his wife struck at him with a bottle she held in her hand, but it did not hit him, falling out of her hand (and it) smashed. Her conduct roused his temper, and he wrested a stake from the hedge close by, and in his blind passion killed the woman almost before he knew what he was about.' (26) His excuses are the excuses of a lot of murderers: the other party initiated the violence, the perpetrator 'lost his head', didn't know what he was doing, and the idea that Ben had to resort to using a hedge stake he just happened to take from the hedge when roused to quell a weaker party, is ludicrous.

Family finally came to visit Ben on the last week, after Ben had asked that they come to see him. On the Thursday his uncle John Hudson and wife Elizabeth came to the goal, and again a newspaper took the chance to lecture on the degeneracy of the colliers, primly reporting that there was no 'display of feeling on the part of any person concerned' (26) (one of Ben's wardens was probably in the pay of the newspapers, or how would they have known?). The paper again slandered the entire collier community by adding that this stoic display was merely 'exemplifying the callous indifference to all serious things, which unhappily is so generally characteristic of the ignorant and debased collier class.' (26) It was not the miners' way to break down in front of others, but those who did not face death daily in the general course of their employment may not have understood this.

On Saturday, with only one clear day before his death, 'quite a troop of friends' (26) came to see Ben, but there were so many that the governor only permitted twelve people access. These were his grandfather, his mother, Mary Vickers (Ben had taken his grandfather's surname when he went to live with him), Henry and Alfred Vickers, two of his brothers and two sisters, Eliza and Ann Vickers, his uncle George Coope and wife, Frederick Vickers, his twin brother and his wife, and John Hudson and wife. Again, papers commented on the lack of emotion shown, and it is interesting that Ben's father, Thomas, didn't visit at all, nor is there any record of him attending the trial. Perhaps he and Ben didn't get on well, which might explain why Ben went to live with his grandfather at such an early age. It could explain also why Ben was not friendly with his own twin brother Frederick who had stayed at home.

Arrangements for Ben's son's future must have been discussed, for afterwards, the prison chaplain wrote a letter for Ben to his brother George:

Derby County Gaols, August 2, 1873

My Dear Brother, – it is my wish that you should have my child George Hudson to bring up, and oh, my dear brother, try your best to train him up in the right way. I hope he will take warning by my sad fate and not give way to evil tempers and passion.

I hereby authorize you to claim and take charge of him and my God bless and reward you for all your kindness to me.

Your unfortunate brother.

I take it very hard that I could not see both George and Polly, for I was as fond of Polly as if she had been my own. Kiss them for me.

BEN. HUDSON (27)

Although he was illiterate, Ben had learnt to print his name, apparently for he had printed his name below the letter. The following day, the Sunday, with less than twenty-four hours left on this earth, Ben wrote another letter to his brother. The prison chaplain seems to have written the letters for him so he could sort out his few affairs, and this letter also enclosed copies of hymns he had chosen to be sung at the services he attended on Sunday, Divine Service and then one in the afternoon, when the Rev. Moore preached a sermon suitable to the occasion that was to occur the next morning. Ben's letter read:

Dear brother,

I enclose a copy of the hymns I chose to be sung today because I think they are very nice ones.

Please to give one to my mother and one each to my sisters and one to Henry, and tell them to keep them for my sake and to learn them by heart, and take particular notice what they say. Give one to my dear boy and kiss him from me, and tell him to be a good boy and to school on Sundays and week-days, and when he becomes a man he will not repent the days of his youth. I wish you to have my gun (here follows some directions of no interest except those concerned to the gun).

I conclude with farewell love to you all, hoping we may meet in a better world.

> *Your sorrowing brother*
> *Benj. Hudson (27)*

Ben also had another letter written and enclosed a lock of his hair, but we don't know to whom this was sent. He had other farewell letters written to a few friends and enclosed copies of the hymn 'Just as I am without one plea.' He then sang a portion of a hymn that he knew, beginning 'We'll face the storm and anchor by and by'. (27)

* * * * *

The Sunday night he did not sleep well, not getting to sleep until one or two in the morning and waking at four. By half-past five he had risen and washed and dressed in prison garb. It was normal for the condemned person to dress in their normal clothes, but Ben had arranged for his mother to have them. Usually, the hangman was given the clothes from the corpse and often would sell them off to the souvenir collector, also offering pieces of the rope used to hang the convicted at a good price. Perhaps this was why Ben did not want the executioner to get his garments. Ben ate some breakfast, a biscuit, bread, a small sherry, and some tea, then waited.

Normally Ben would have been taken straight from his cell to the gallows shed, but he was being housed in a cell in the old debtor's prison, so it seems that at some stage he was transferred through the yard to a cell closer, for he was taken through the yard, and, unusually, 'the whole of the male prisoners were drawn up in the exercise yard, and the prisoner passed before them, waving his hand as a last farewell.' (26) Ben saw five prisoners there whom he had met with at the assizes, and whom he had known from the Handley neighbourhood, and he asked that he be allowed to go over to them, shake hands and say goodbye. This was allowed. It had rained softly all night, but as the hour approached eight o'clock, the time of the execution, it had started to rain heavily, and a fog had come up over the town. Inside the gaol, a reporter said, 'Silence, painful almost in its intensity, reigned everywhere.' (5)

Marwood the executioner had arrived in Derby on Saturday. A master shoemaker from Horncastle, this was to be his second execution, and Ben would be given a quicker and less painful death than if he had been served by Calcraft, the previous hangman. Marwood had introduced the 'long drop' from Ireland, which severed the spinal cord and gave a quick, clean death, rather than Calcraft's shoddy stranglings on the end of a short rope, which could often prolong death for many agonising minutes. Marwood had tested out the gallows, just inside the main portal and declared all sound. It was the old gallows which had been last been used some eleven years before, standing about four feet from the ground, with the open space below covered over, save for an aperture to allow Marlow to pull the lever which released the trapdoor on which Hudson would stand. The rope, about six feet in length, was fixed to an iron crossbar, supported by two upright iron bars, the knot on the bottom end being a slip knot. A short pair of steps at one end led onto the scaffold.

At a quarter to eight the under-sheriff of Derbyshire and a sheriff's officer entered the goal and formally demanded the body of Benjamin Hudson. The three-quarter chimes began, then a funeral bell began to chime dolorously within the prison. Chosen press reporters were admitted and waited at some distance from the scaffold.

At a few minutes to eight o'clock Hudson was conducted to a small office about 200 yards from the gallows, where Marwood, 'who was dressed in a rather shabby suit of black cloth… small in stature, wiry-looking and middle-aged,' (5) formally asked him if his name was Benjamin Hudson. Ben replied yes and Marwood pinioned his arms with leather straps. As the chimes of eight began on the prison clock, a procession set out from the scaffold. The gaol chaplain and the condemned man went first, the chaplain wearing a black gown and carrying a prayer book, Hudson with his prison cap in his right hand and a bouquet of wild flowers in his hand which had been brought by his aunt on Saturday, and which he had asked to be allowed to carry to his death. Behind Ben and the priest came the hangman, followed by the Under-Sheriff, Sheriff's Officer, the Governor of the prison, then the gaol surgeon and another surgeon, and six wardens. The rest of the execution is probably best left to a journalist who was there to describe:

'The culprit walked to the foot of the scaffold with his eyes fixed on the ground, but he did not betray the slightest emotion, and mounted the steps leading to the platform with a firm tread, the chaplain meanwhile reading the burial service by his side with a faltering voice. As soon as he stepped upon the drop the hangman pinioned his feet, and he stood quietly looking about the prison yard until the executioner drew the white cap over his head and face. Even then he did not evince any agitation... The hangman, after fastening his feet together, quickly adjusted the noose around his neck, and, after drawing it tight... took his place at the lever... It was now eight o'clock exactly, and before the clock had finished striking the executioner pressed the lever which shot the bolt from under the drop – a sort of trap door – and the unfortunate man dangled at the end of the rope to all intents lifeless. The bouquet of flowers fell from his left hand as soon as he dropped, but his prison cap remained in his other hand.... The length of the drop was four feet and a half.... From his first appearance on the fatal scene to the final portion of the dread ceremony he did not utter a word or tremble in the least degree – thus carrying out his resolution to display his usual characteristic fortitude and firmness to the end.' (26)

There were several contradictory accounts of how swiftly Ben died. The *Derby Mercury* recorded that 'After he fell his body was motionless for a few seconds, but his chest distended to a great size, and his hands, arms and legs twitched slightly several times. He died in two minutes and a half, apparently quite easily.' (26) The *Manchester Evening News* made it 'easily, in three minutes', (28) another gave death occurring 'immediately the bolt fell', (29) while a Liverpool paper claimed, 'He seemed to die a very hard death, having struggled at least four minutes.' (30) These seem strange discrepancies, and maybe it wasn't as clean a death as the Long Drop method later gave once it was perfected. After all, this was only Marlow's second execution. Perhaps the different accounts are because only six reporters witnessed the death from a distance, accounts in many papers were written from telegraphed reports sent by 'stringers' who sent the basic facts as they saw them, and additions were made by other journalists in a macabre 'Chinese Whispers' game.

The black flag unfurled above Derby Gaol, a sign that the execution had taken place. The body was left to hang for an hour, as was the custom, and was then cut down and placed in a plain pine coffin, awaiting the Coroner's Inquest. This took place by order of a new law and was the first time in Derbyshire such an inquest had been conducted. At twelve o'clock a in the Governor's private office a jury was duly sworn and then shown Ben's body in its coffin:

'The face and hands were white and cold as marble. The arms were placed at the body's side, and on the breast were deposited the prisoner's cap and the bouquet which he had held when the fatal bolt was drawn. The mouth was partially open, and the lips had a lived hue. The face appeared slightly swollen, but the neck did not bear much outward evidence of dislocation.' (26)

The jury duly returned a verdict that Benjamin Hudson, capitally convicted of the crime of wilful murder, came by his death by hanging, according to the law. Outside in the prison grounds, close by the gallows and the prison wall, a grave had been prepared by convicts, and the coffin in which Ben lay was placed in the ground and quick lime spread inside. Benjamin Hudson was finally free from the torments and passions that had destroyed him. He was buried in an unmarked grave.

So, ironically, was Eliza Hudson. She is in Handley Churchyard, but there is no marking stone, no memorial. Until the late 1970's there was a custom to leave the piece of land where Eliza was so cruelly attacked and killed unploughed, in her memory, as a mark of respect, something she got little of during her sad, short life. Eventually, the farm changed hands, became a private residence, and even the stile and lane have now gone, and there is only a bend in the footpath to show where Ben lost his mind and Eliza her life.

REFERENCES

1. 'Handley Church – a Poetic Memorial', by John Holland,
   privately printed pamphlet 1845
2. The *Sheffield and Rotherham Independent*, Monday 3rd May 1873
3. The *Derbyshire Times and Chesterfield Herald*, Wednesday 30th April 1873
4. The *Sheffield Daily Telegraph*, Thursday 1st May 1873
5. The *Sheffield and Rotherham Independent*, Tuesday 5th August 1873
6. The *Sheffield Daily Telegraph*, Monday 3rd June 1872
7. The *Derbyshire Times and Chesterfield Herald*, Saturday 3rd May 1873
8. The *Sheffield and Rotherham Independent*, Thursday 1st May 1873
9. The *Derbyshire Times and Chesterfield Herald*, Wednesday July 16th 1873
10. The *Sheffield Daily Telegraph*, Saturday 26th April 1873
11. The *Sheffield and Rotherham Independent*, Wednesday 16th 1873
12. The *Huntly Express*, Saturday May 10th 1873
13. The *Sheffield and Rotherham Independent*, Friday 2nd May 1873
14. The *Illustrated Police News*, Saturday 3rd May 1873
15. The *Sheffield and Rotherham Independent*, Saturday 17th May 1873
16. The Derby Mercury, Wednesday 30th April 1873
17. The Sheffield and Rotherham Independent, Monday 28th April 1873
18. The *Newry Reporter*, Saturday 10th May 1873
19. The *Burton Chronicle*, Thursday 8th May 1873
20. *The Independent Collier: Some Recent Studies of Nineteenth Century*
    Coalmining Communities in Britain and the United States,
    by J.H.M. Laslett, U.C.L.A. 1982
21. The *Derbyshire Times and Chesterfield Herald*, Saturday 10th April 1873
22. The *Sheffield and Rotherham Independent*, Wednesday 7th May 1873
23. The *Sheffield and Rotherham Independent*, Monday 12th May 1873
24. The *Sheffield Daily Telegraph*, Wednesday 16th June 1873
25. The *Derbyshire Courier*, Saturday 2nd August 1873
26. The *Derby Mercury*, Wednesday 6th August 1873
27. The *Derbyshire Times and Chesterfield Herald*, 9th August 1873
28. The *Manchester Evening News*, Monday 4th April 1873
29. The *Greenock Telegraph and Clyde Shipping Gazette*, Monday 4th April 1873
30. The *Liverpool Mercury*, Tuesday 5th August 1873

MATLOCK'S BLOODIEST MURDER
THE MYSTERY OF BALMORAL HOUSE
Richard Litchfield

ISBN 978-1-910489-73-4   Price: **£7.50**

Available at all good book shops, from the publisher at:

www.countrybooks.biz or from Amazon

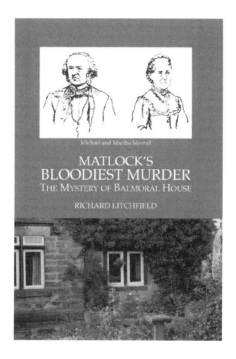

The Matlock Mystery, as it was called, is perhaps Matlock's bloodiest, and most intriguing murder. An old woman, savagely killed in a remote house one dark, snowy night in 1891 on the moors above Matlock, no seeming motive, no clues. It was the sensation of the day, both locally and nationally, and the story has never been told fully before.

Richard Litchfield, who has studied and researched the murder for over twenty years, now tells the story in fascinating, unflinching detail, and points the finger squarely at the person responsible. It is a remarkable account of a very strange murder which deserves to be better known in the annals of true crime.